TUDOR HOUSES

TUDOR HOUSES

MICHAEL WALSH

ILLUSTRATIONS BY RICHARD TOGLIA

A ROUNDTABLE PRESS BOOK

 HOME PLANNERS, INC.

A Roundtable Press Book

Directors: Marsha Melnick, Susan E. Meyer

Assistant Editor: Marguerite Ross

Illustrations and Interior Design: Richard Toglia

Book and Cover Design: Michaelis/Carpelis
Design Associates, Inc.

Photography: Jessie Walker: frontispiece and
pages 16, 21, 22, 24, 29, 31; Hedrich Blessing:
page 19; The Alderman Company: page 27

Designs for Interior Photographs: frontispiece,
Lynn Keck Petty, ASID; page 17, Janet Schirn;
page 21, Mary Southworth; pages 22 and 31,
Jeffrey Lawrence

Published by Home Planners, Inc.
23761 Research Drive
Farmington Hills, Michigan 48024

Charles W. Talcott, Chairman
Rickard Bailey, President and Publisher
Karin Lotarski, Production Editor

First printing, April 1989

ISBN: 0-918894-66-2

TUDOR HOME STYLES

🐦 If you're searching for a home that looks solid and substantial, that sends clear emotional messages about traditional values and conveys a sense of permanence, place, and price, look no further. 🐦 Tudor home styles embody all these sought-after traits, and more. 🐦 Although it is derived from centuries-old English prototypes, the Tudor-style house has become the epitome of the all-American home, an integral part of our architectural heritage. 🐦 Yet Tudor style is not ancient architecture but living history. 🐦 It is a recognition that tradition is not trapped in time but is something that remains relevant generation after generation. 🐦 In the pages ahead you'll discover how Tudor style has stood the test of time and why it's as right for the present as it was for the past.

TABLE OF ONTENTS

TUDOR HOME STYLES

Good Bone Structure:
An Inherited Trait 9

Material Matters:
A Masterful Mix 11

Character Builders:
Doors and Windows 13

Home Is Where the Hearth Is:
The Towering Tudor Chimney . . . 14

TUDOR HOME DECORATING IDEAS

The Tudor Entry Hall 16

The Great Room 18

An Upstairs Bedroom 20

Fine Dining 22

A Heart-of-the-Home Kitchen 24

The Personal Spa 26

A Kitchen That Cooks 28

The Library-Den 30

HOME PLANS

Cottages 32
Villas 96
Manors 168

How to Read Floor Plans 198
How to Choose a Contractor 199
Ordering Your Plans 200

Index to Plans 208

 olid, substantial, and self-assured, the Tudor house has been the one that generations of upwardly mobile Americans have consistently aspired to. From medieval times on, it has been a desired symbol of achievement, a live-in reward for effort, enterprise, and, eventually, success.

Tudor-style achitecture in America, prior to this century, was primarily reserved for what would later be regarded as architectural landmarks, the huge mansions occupied by the moguls of the new industrial age, or even mammoth clubhouses at exclusive country clubs. But with the rise of the middle class, the style's popularity spread. By the 1920s, Tudor was so closely associated with economic achievement and conservative good taste that it was commonly known as "Stockbroker Tudor." Eventually, it became almost universally regarded as the house of choice among those who had an option—so much so that today there is hardly a city or suburb in America without a neighborhood comprised largely of Tudor-style homes.

While the stereotypical American starter home may have been a cozy, vine-covered cottage with a white picket fence, for move-up buyers the Tudor house has long been the culmination of the American dream. These days, however, Tudor style is more accessible and affordable than ever, even for first-time home buyers. Because it is a style that is adaptable and appropriate for any size home, Tudor's appeal has never been so widespread as it is today.

And that's saying a lot, because the Tudor house has had a long and distinguished history. Architectural historians trace its beginnings to early sixteenth-century England. Because of political, social, and economic changes, fortresslike castles were on the way out. The increased wealth of the merchant class and large landholders gave rise to the development of smaller but still very grand manor houses and country estates. Because these houses, which shared distinctive architectural characteristics, evolved during the reign of the royal Tudors (Henry VII, Henry VIII, Edward VI, Mary, and Elizabeth), the style came to be known as Tudor. Later, even English cottages were designed in the Tudor image.

But it's important to remember that the Tudor house developed during what histo-

GOOD BONE STRUCTURE: AN INHERITED TRAIT

in with brick, stone, or stucco. Colonists brought this technique to America but discovered it was unsuitable in harsh New England winters, because it was hard keeping the filled-in sections weathertight. Still, the tradition of half-timbering persisted. Eventually, however, it evolved into a decorative device applied after the framing had been covered by a continuous wraparound surface of brick, wood, stucco, or stone.

Nothing more distinguishes a Tudor house from other styles that the exposed wooden timbers seemingly embedded into the home's facade. What appears to be a strong wooden skeleton is one of the reasons a Tudor home looks so substantial and solid.

Now a decorative, applied detail that visibly ties Tudor present to Tudor past, "half-timbering" was originally an innovative building technique. While the structural members of typical American wood-framed houses are usually concealed, English Tudor houses had the spaces between the timber framing filled

Today's Tudor home, then, is the result of modern, energy-efficient, New World construction techniques and Old World character. Exposed half-timbers, applied vertically, horizontally, diagonally, and sometimes slightly arched, are still the most popular elements on Tudor-style homes.

rians call the Early Renaissance, a period of transition between 1500 and 1650, not just for England but for European civilization. National boundaries and national characters came to be more or less established after centuries of war. Economic prosperity spread rapidly. International trade was followed by the exchange of cultural influences between nations. The inspiration for architectural detail and interior decoration was imported and exported as readily as was merchandise.

And England, already a melting-pot culture, was at the center of this cultural revolution. The ships of this seafaring nation tied England to the Orient, as well as to the Continent. Consequently, Tudor architecture was for the most part a product of international influences. Even today, you can see in a Tudor house traces of Gothic windows, classic Roman doorways, German and English exposed timber framing, and touches of Swiss chalet exterior ornamentation.

Is it any wonder then that America, a nation of mixed ancestry with particularly close ties to the British Empire, would embrace what would eventually become known as English Tudor style? You don't have to be a blueblood to see your ancestral roots in the shape and features of a Tudor house. It is an instantly recognizable and comfortingly familiar style. Even in our seemingly rootless and highly mobile so-

ciety, we recognize that a Tudor house embodies our heritage, marries the present to the past, and yields a sense of continuity that few other home styles can rival.

In America, the arrival of Tudor-style architecture coincided with the arrival of the Puritans and the first German settlers. They brought with them a building technique known as half-timbering, which became a standard feature of Tudor architecture that can still be seen on most Tudor homes today.

But it wasn't until the country began moving from an agrarian era into the industrial age that Tudor homes found firm footing on American soil. From about 1890 to 1910, the style was largely known as Elizabethan, because it mimicked English cottages built during the reign of Queen Elizabeth I (1558–1603). (This style was revived in late nineteenth-century England by architect Richard Norman Shaw.) At first, Tudor's most discernible features—half-timbering, massive chimneys, and Gothic windows—were adapted to American Queen Anne-style houses (also based on English models twenty years old). But soon Tudor began to imitate the authentic English historical style with more accuracy and eventually became known as English Tudor style. By the 1920s, the Tudor style had become a permanent part of the American architectural landscape.

In the decades since then, America has done to Tudor architecture what it has always done to customs, fashions, and styles originating elsewhere. Rather than blindly following precedents established in England and Europe, American architects and builders adapted the style to American needs and sensibilities. They married history to the here and now. Their goal—now as well as then—was to approximate, not to duplicate. That's why today you may com-

MATERIAL MATTERS: A MASTERFUL MIX

If you find Tudor-style architecture appealing but have always preferred a house in brick, wood, stucco, or even stone, you can have the best of all possible worlds: Tudor style and *varied* materials.

One of Tudor style's most enduring traditions has been and continues to be the use of multiple exterior cladding materials. Although a single material such as brick may dominate any given house, a second material (say, stucco) appears in generous quantities. Frequently, a third material, perhaps a stone, provides architectural detail around doors, windows, or entryways.

The combinations seem un-limited: stucco with brick, stone with stucco, brick with wood shingles, wood with stucco.

In recent years, Tudor styling has been increasingly applied to more conventional American-style houses, particularly the split-level and the Ranch. However, the liberal mix of exterior materials used to build these adaptations continues to keep them firmly within the Tudor tradition.

monly find Tudor-style detailing applied to a house that in shape resembles other American favorites such as Cape Cods, Ranches, or even split-levels.

In fact, Tudor's eclectic character probably accounts most for its undiminished popularity. Unlike other architectural styles associated almost exclusively with specific regions of the country—the New England Saltbox or the Cape Cod, say, or the Midwestern bungalow, the Spanish-style houses of the Southwest, or the South's Greek Revival plantation houses—the Tudor house is at home from coast to coast and border to border. It has adapted so thoroughly that it nearly always looks

appropriate and suited to its site.

Of course, part of the Tudor style's adaptability is due to its still discernible English accents: the decorative half-timbers, the steeply pitched rooflines, the familiar front-facing gables, the varied eave lines, the massive chimneys, and the distinctive windows and doors. These features—formal, stately, historically evocative and graphic—rarely look out of place.

More important, perhaps, is that the materials used in building a Tudor-style house make it seem indigenous to most areas. These materials are almost always earthy and organic. Typically, the building formula relies on wood, brick, stone, or stucco applied more often than not, in combinations of two, three, or four.

Consequently, Tudor-style houses may display the visible half-timbers and stuccoing of Mission-style houses of the West, the red brick of Atlantic Coast row houses, or quarried stone, clapboard siding, or even

CHARACTER BUILDERS: DOORS AND WINDOWS

When it comes to architectural embellishment, few other home styles offer such distinctive and diverse details as the Tudor home. Although its decorative half-timbering and steeply pitched gables define and dominate the style, much of the Tudor home's eclectic

character and cottage charm come from its doors and windows.

Often based on medieval precedent, front entries frequently feature traditional solid-wood, board-and-battenlike front doors, sometimes with exposed wrought-

iron hinges. More often than not, these are flanked by full-length multipane sidelights that help keep foyers light and bright. On some Tudor home adaptations the front doorway is framed with a brick or cut-stone arch that evokes Renaissance architectural detailing. Covered front porches—sometimes created by re-

cessing the entryway beneath the roofline—are also popular.

Tudor-style windows are instantly recognizable because of their multiple square- or diamond-shaped panes reminiscent of the leaded windows in Gothic cathedrals and ancient English manor houses. Often grouped into

strings of three or more, Tudor windows bring abundant natural light into the house. For people looking out, the divided panes create a sense of security that large expanses of glass cannot match.

Also common are tall, narrow bay windows; oriels (projecting windows supported by wooden brackets); windows set into roof dormers; and windows topped with transoms.

From inside or out, the windows and doors of a Tudor home

are not just standard elements. They are deliberately decorative features that contribute significantly to the style's distinctive personality.

HOME IS WHERE THE HEARTH IS: THE TOWERING TUDOR CHIMNEY

. . . .

Tudor architecture dates to the sixteenth century, but one of its most distinctive features—the often massive and elaborate chimney—reaches back an additional 200 years to the English

castles of the late Middle Ages. In them the fireplace as we know it today first appeared and, along with it, the chimney.

Until the mid-1300s, a fireplace in Gothic structures was more like a fire pit, often located in the center of the great central halls. Smoke from the fire simply drifted upward in these huge rooms with high ceilings and out through a hole in the roof. But

then the fireplace was moved to a side wall and topped with a projecting hood that siphoned the smoke out through a stone chimney.

That may not seem like much of an architectural achievement,

but the relocation of the fireplace, the development and refinement of the chimney, and the subsequent clearing of interior air would eventually change the way all houses were designed. It meant that a second-story floor could be added to the huge central spaces and could be heated by its own fireplace. It also meant more efficient use of space on all floors, because a major obstacle had been moved.

By the time the Tudor era dawned (about 1500, according to most architectural historians), the

chimney was no longer just a functional feature, but a decorative and symbolic one as well. Typically, the Tudor chimney was—and is—a prominent ar-

chitectural feature. Often, it contained several flues from multiple fireplaces. Even when there was only a single fireplace, Tudor chimneys were often topped with two or three cylindrical clay chimney pots that suggested multiple fireplaces—symbols, at the time, of status and prosperity.

The Tudor chimney tradition remains a favorite architectural element, as symbolic of home and hearth now as it was 500 years ago. Unusually tall and massive, the chimney is often positioned

prominently at the front or side of a house. Frequently, the lower part of the chimney may feature complex patterns of brick, stone, or a combination of the two.

And, although clay chimney pots are relatively rare these days, many Tudor-style chimneys are still topped with two flue openings—one for a real fireplace and one for a more recent innovation: the gas-fired, forced-air furnace.

yards—all of which blur the distinction between indoors and outdoors. Inside, of course, the Tudor house is what you want it to be: toe-the-line traditional, charm-filled country, or sleek and sophisticated contemporary. As you'll discover on the following pages, the Tudor style's typical interior features are as diverse and delightful as its exterior ones.

New England wood shingles. The most distinctive characteristic of traditional Tudor architecture is that, no matter what the combination, these various materials are sensitively and seamlessly melded into a well-integrated and visually pleasing whole that rarely fails to set Tudor-style homes apart from their all-wood, all-brick, all-stone, or all-stucco counterparts.

When it comes to natural materials, imaginatively and effectively intermingled, the Tudor style offers the best of all possible worlds. What's more, the Tudor-style home's largely organic substances tie it intimately to its natural surroundings—trees, rocks, and the earth. Invariably, a Tudor-style house looks so natural in its setting that it seems as though it grew out of the environment itself.

To make the most of this well-rooted illusion, you'll find that many Tudor-style houses offer covered porches (at the front, side, or rear), entryways pulled back below a roofline, bay windows, second-story dormer windows, and even balconies and court-

Often, you'll find exposed-wood ceiling beams, slate, brick or stone entryways, and prominent fireplaces with brick, stone, or wood mantels. Wood paneling and wainscoting are also common in Tudor homes, as are window seats, dramatic center-hall stairways, and cathedral ceilings. Far from dictating interior ambience, however, Tudor architecture easily lends itself to nearly any preference. This simply means that a Tudor house is as accommodating and adaptable on the inside as it is on the outside.

Because you get only one chance to make a good first impression, an entryway that signals hospitality and graciousness is vital. The continuing presence of the entry hall in Tudor style homes tells us that there still exists an appreciation for a once-standard home feature, and acknowledges that a properly engineered entry hall can be a functional as well as a ceremonial space. In two-story homes, this is often where a grand staircase is located. The entry hall is also often a pivot point that eliminates the need for multiple interior hallways. And the coat closet,

. . . .

An entranceway is an introduction to your home. It can be as formal or casual as suits you. In addition to being a hospitable place to greet guests, an entrance hall can be a hard-working room, designed as much for function as for effect. And details—a coat tree, an umbrella stand, a small table that provides a place for parcels and mail— mean a lot.

another common-sense feature often left out of modern homes, is found here. Visually, the character of an entry hall sets the tone for the character of your entire home. Rich with authentic Tudor-style interior architecture— half-timbered walls, beamed ceiling, plaster infill, an open staircase, and Tudor arches above the door and window (*photo opposite*)—an ample entry hall's furnishings (mostly English antiques) occupy the perimeter of the room, emphasizing the entry's dimensions. Abundant woodwork and hardwood floors convey character and warmth.

With two trim, tailored sofas, an entry hall (*top*) doubles as an intimate sitting room. A soft-hued color scheme and area rugs counterbalance imposing architecture.

A mix of furniture styles—traditional, antique, and contemporary—gives an entrance hall (*bottom*) an eclectic look. Stenciled or painted walls add color and pattern, and a hall table and chandelier provide a focal point.

s stately as any grand English manor house, an accommodating great room (*photo opposite*) puts an invigorating mix of furniture styles into a traditional Tudor context. Exposed rafters and beams, painted in an eggshell shade, provide a light topping for a room comprised largely of rich, dark woods, including such Tudor trademarks as hardwood floors, oak paneling, dentil moldings, cornices, and decorative pilasters. A fabulous Chinese coromandel screen and Oriental accessories live in harmony with French and English furnishings. Multiple furniture groupings serve as distinct yet compatible zones.

Less architecturally ornate, but no less inviting than the interior shown in the photograph, a variation on the great

No longer just a ceremonial and symbolic room, a great room can, with multiple furniture groupings, cater to a crowd or coddle a couple.

room theme (*top*) features a leather-topped game table and four upholstered French side chairs on one side of the room and a sofa/love seat/wing chair sitting area on the other. Simple but elegant straight-hanging draperies flank Gothic-style window-panes.

Performance lives up to promise in a great room that serves as both a living area and

a dining area (*bottom*). Bleached oak walls provide a more countrified backdrop for formal furnishings, including an antique English chaise longue and a striking antique English secretary. Here, color is the unifying factor: blue for dining chairs and chaise, peach for armchair and skirted table, pale green for sofas and ceiling—all derived from a delicate, floral-patterned area rug.

thanks to the Tudor style's steeply pitched roofs and multiple gables, a second-story room often has what amounts to a vaulted ceiling. This architectural bonus gives extra character to interior spaces. An upstairs bedroom can function as a multi-purpose room. Reserve space for an attractive bookcase or an armoire that conceals a television.

The strong vertical lines of whitewashed pine paneling and the slender turned posts of a reproduction antique four-poster bed (*photo opposite*) help to stretch the room visually from floor to ceiling. Although the quantity of furnishings and accessories is limited, the overscaled bed and plentiful cabbage-rose chintz fabric give the bedroom a look of

. . . .

Designed for twenty-four-hour comfort, a bedroom can be more than just a place to sleep. With the addition of just one sizable armchair or loveseat, a bedroom can be a private retreat long before the sun goes down.

English country abundance.

With the generous folds of a satin canopy cascading from wall-mounted wood poles to form a backdrop for a painted daybed, this bedroom (*top*) has a distinctly French Empire flavor. But strong English accents abound in a dresser with spiral-turned details, an antique table, and an ample overstuffed,

rolled-arm easy chair. A pale yellow ceiling gives the room a sunny disposition.

Enhancing a bedroom's horizontal dimensions (*bottom*), a high, bracketed shelf under a sky-blue ceiling provides a place for books and prized possessions. Underneath, a compartmented built-in with stenciled doors serves as a headboard for twin-sized guest beds.

o offset the eat-and-run lives many people lead, dining rooms should be designed for the special occasions when we can relax for more than a few moments with family or a few close friends.

Classic Chippendale chairs, a striking Oriental rug, and a long, polished wood table are the quintessential ingredients for a traditional formal dining room (*photo opposite*). Painted wood cornice moldings and low wainscoting add architectural interest, and wallpaper lends soft color and subtle pattern to a room that makes any meal a stately occasion.

For a look somewhere between manor house and farmhouse, a round, gate-legged dining table and sturdy, country-style chairs yield a dining room with informal

rural warmth (*top*). The table's natural wood top and painted legs make it both rustic and refined. Leather and wood chairs recall the furnishings of English taverns, where comfort and conviviality rivaled cuisine.

Hunter-green walls, often found in English country homes, silhouette a dining room's furniture and display its architectural features—windows, woodwork, and painted fireplace (*bottom*). The carved melon shapes on the antique table's legs were a favorite form on Tudor-era furnishings. Contemporary cane-backed chairs prove that contrast can be as effective as compatibility: The unexpected mix of old and new creates a one-of-a-kind look.

. . . .

A dining room should provide an ambience that actually promotes lingering and stimulates a feeling of togetherness. Fine furnishings, beautiful textiles, and rich colors and patterns should be on the menu. A dining room can nourish the spirit as well as the body.

 Today's kitchen is typically the hub around which household life revolves. In newer homes the kitchen is part of a suite of rooms including a dining room and family room. Because it's often visible from other areas, the kitchen has to be more decoratively compatible than ever before.

With pumpkin-colored walls, raised-panel cabinet doors of dark-stained wood, an island topped with butcher block, and a vintage brass light fixture, this kitchen is a traditional eye-opener (*photo opposite*).

. . . .

Buttery yellow and French-toast browns yield a kitchen that is both light and warm. Copper accents enhance the French flavor.

. . . .

The colors of country gingham and Dutch-style tile soften a kitchen's high-tech appliances and mask its hard-working nature. A central island doubles as a buffet and augments counter space.

Ceramic tile, used as a backsplash and as wainscoting, provides color and pattern, yet is durable and easy to clean. Although they probably date only to the Victorian era, the salvaged leaded- and stained-glass windows here mimic the Tudor style's leaded windows.

Stained-wood cabinets, mosaic tile, and butter-yellow walls give a leaner, lighter ambience (*top*). Maple butter-block countertops tie the sink and cooktop to the island, which features open shelving on one side for quick, easy access to frequently used stockpots, kitchen ware, and serving bowls. Except for a ruffled valance over the sink, the diamond-paned windows have been left unadorned.

Another kitchen (*bottom*) takes on Dutch Colonial character with pale blue bead board cabinets (often used for ceilings on vintage Victorian porches), glossy white, Delftlike ceramic tile (on countertops and walls), and classic blue-and-white porcelain pieces that are both functional and decorative.

Bathrooms are bigger, better, and more luxurious than ever. Today's bath is a place for pampering and for soothing jangled nerves. The locker-room look of the past no longer works. By using today's enormous range of decorative and durable materials, the bathroom can become every bit as attractive as the rest of the house.

State-of-the-art bath fixtures will give us convenience, but comfort is visual and emotional, not just functional. Exposed wood beams and posts certainly have Tudor connotations, but when combined with a miniprint wall covering and coordinating fabric they take on an all-American, country-style character (*photo opposite*). The warm woods and milk-chocolate-colored fixtures cozy up to white ceramic tile.

Or is it the rustic elegance of a French farmhouse you want? The chateauesque architecture of such a setting is already in place (*top*). Pale amethyst walls, blue and white ceramic tile,

and gold-plated bathtub hardware enhance the French country home personality. A gilt-framed mirror adds old gold to the provincial mix.

Drawing on the American Southwest for inspiration, this bath (*bottom*) reflects America's arid desert areas, with earthy, Mexican clay tiles, plastered walls painted in adobe hues, sun-bleached wood beams and posts, Indian-blanket shower curtains, and a Navajo rug. A cactus-green bathtub, commode, and sink are cool-color counterpoints.

· · · · · · · · · · · · · · · · · · · ·

Evocative of French porcelain, blue-and-white ceramic tiles and wooden beams give a bath French country flair that is simultaneously rustic and refined.

· · · · · · · · · · · · · · · · · · · ·

Desert colors, native American patterns, and earthy textures lend the look of the Southwest to Tudor-style architecture, demonstrating once again Tudor's adaptable nature.

By nature, a kitchen is a utilitarian space. You don't have to sacrifice a kitchen's heart-warming character for eat-and-run efficiency, though.

Chock full of charm and homey warmth, a kitchen with honey-colored cabinets and patterned wallpaper that evokes imported tile (*photo opposite*) is a memorable place to prepare meals. Some of its less obvious features, which make kitchen duty easier and more attractive, include:
• Extra-wide counters cantilevered beyond stock base cabinets to provide more work surface.
• A ceiling-mounted pot rack. Pots and pans come out of the dishwasher or sink and go directly to an easy-to-reach pot rack for instant accessibility from the cooktop.
• Glass cabinet

. . . .

Tile-like wallpaper or do-it-yourself stencils infuse a kitchen with color, pattern, and charm. Decorative cabinet hardware—think of it as room jewelry—adds refined, fine-tuned detail, and wood adds warmth.

doors. Because you can see through them, they make the kitchen seem larger than it is.

In a lighter, brighter variation (*top*), cupboard doors are inset with mirrors that not only add the sparkle of cut crystal to the room but also create an illusion of spaciousness. Tying inside to out, green plastic laminate-topped counters pick up similar shades just

outside the generous windows. Raised-panel base cabinet doors are a traditional favorite.

Hand-stenciled designs traced around Tudor-style windows, terra-cotta tile countertops, and tongue-and-groove wood cabinet doors give another kitchen a hand-crafted look (*bottom*). Creamy yellow walls keep the room light and are easy on the eyes.

raditional decorating is not limited to a single look or to a single period or style. Instead, it is a decorating style as versatile as the Tudor house itself.

The epitome of a toe-the-line, traditional Tudor-style room, a library-den (*photo opposite*) features a generous, curved bay window, decorative plaster ceiling, fireplace with Tudor arch, and Elizabethan oak-paneled walls. Also traditional and timeless are tufted black leather club chairs, a vivid Oriental rug, and a game table with four French chairs. The idea is to make these spaces especially accommodating to those who live in the house.

A contemporary sofa upholstered in a tartan plaid, an am-

ple wing chair, and "inlaid" wallpaper give a second version of the same room more of an English country ambience (*top*). Bright colors and patterns contribute to the casual character. A straightforward treatment nicely dresses the window.

Pale blue paneling and white woodwork around the ample windows give this room (*bottom*) the

look of fine Wedgwood china—still traditional, but lighter and softer. The gentle curves of the reproduction furnishings—including a Louis XV sofa, a pair of seventeenth-century Spanish armchairs, and a French writing desk—contrast nicely with the paneling's rectangular motif. A grand piano allows the room to function as a music room as well as den.

. . . .

All the comforts of home—a bay window, crackling fire, and shelves stocked with well-thumbed books—are found in a room that is simultaneously a den, library, music room, and family room.

COTTAGES

A fixture in American neighborhoods for more than half a century, the Tudor cottage is more popular now than ever. The understated charm of the architecture continues to convey coziness and a sense of stability.

Plan 2806, page 44

Single floor:

1,208 square feet

he ideal Tudor cottage, adapted for suburban living, is relatively small in scale and size—yet it offers many of the amenities and architectural detailing found in much larger floor plans. Living room and dining room are combined here, with both spaces enjoying the luxury of the fireplace and accessibility to the rear terrace. The dining room even includes a built-in china cabinet. The kitchen work triangle layout now accepted as good design can be seen here, as well as in the other plans. In addition to cabinet storage in the kitchen, a pantry and broom closet are also located here, as is a comfortable-sized eating area. Upon entering the living room, visitors have a view to the rear terrace and garden. The facade's traditional Tudor details include tall, narrow windows accented by diamond-shaped panes repeated on the small window of the front door, a gable dovecote located above the garage door, and decorative oversized hinges on the garage and front door. An optional basement plan is also available.

A bay window in the eating area of the kitchen, its window treatment kept to a minimum, makes for a cheerful, light-filled room.

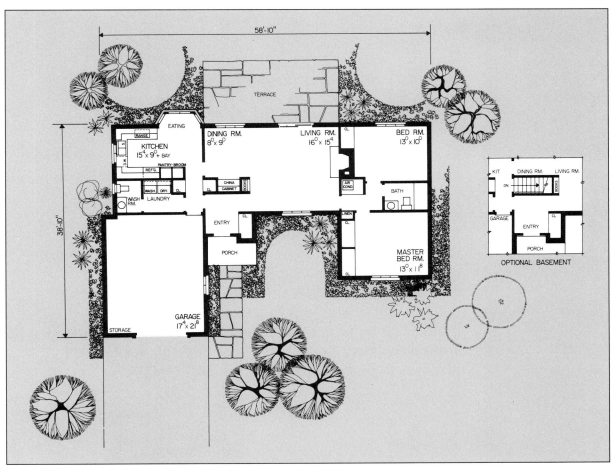

Single floor:

1,176 square feet

 Just because a house is small doesn't mean it can't still offer many of the amenities of a larger home. This house is a good example. Outside, much traditional Tudor detailing is in evidence. These familiar features are enhanced by the introduction of more contemporary elements, such as a pair of window boxes on either side of the front entrance. Because today's busy schedules leave many living rooms and dining rooms largely unused anyway, this floor plan boldly eliminates both. Replacing them is a gathering room, a large space with a raised hearth, which also incorporates a dining area. In warm weather the adjacent terrace can function as almost another room. The family's more informal meals can be planned around the kitchen nook. This compact floor plan still manages to include three bedrooms.

Stenciling can add a personalized touch to any room. From the breakfast table in the kitchen nook, anyone can appreciate the charm of this popular painting technique.

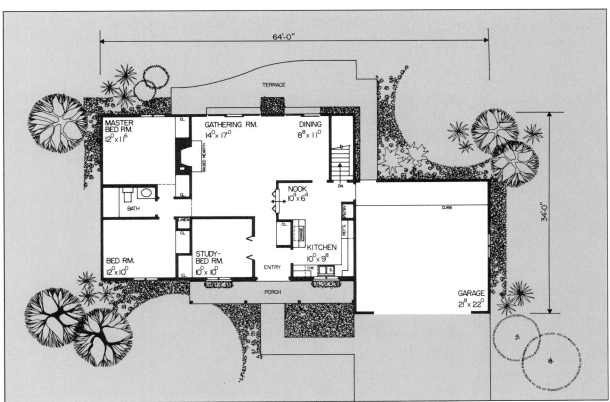

Single floor:
1,499 square feet

reaking with tradition, this floor plan places the living room at the rear of the house instead of the front. In this case, however, the location is ideal, because it takes advantage of window views of the rear garden, with its gently curved terrace. For formal entertaining this plan is quite practical. From the entrance hall guests have immediate access to either the living room or dining room. On the other hand, family members can enjoy casual meals or just relax in the combination kitchen and family room, which is divided by an area large enough to accommodate a breakfast-room table. Bedrooms, including a master suite, are located on the other side of the house. An optional basement plan allows for the addition of more recreation and hobby space. Such distinguishing features of Tudor architecture as the round chimney pot and patterned brickwork on the front of the house are in evidence here. Tudor detailing even extends to the garage, with its steeply pitched roof and projecting ornamental gable.

Informal seating is provided in the dining room, which has a window seat overlooking the entrance courtyard. This location would also be ideal for displaying plants.

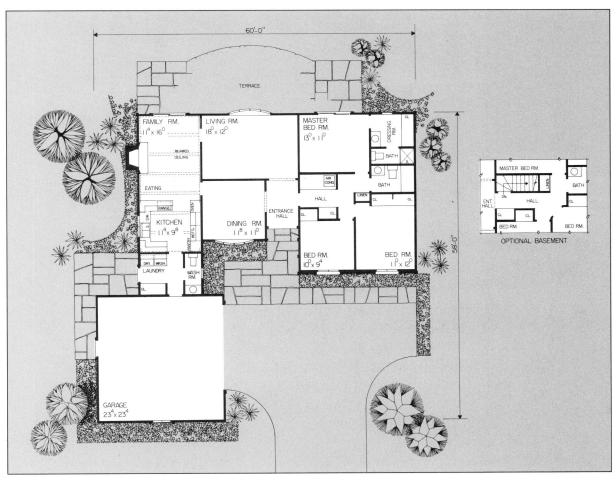

Single floor:
1,540 square feet

 Today's family, used to entertaining informally, often finds itself neglecting one room in the house in particular: the dining room. This floor plan eliminates the room entirely and instead incorporates a space for dining in the large living room. Adjacent to this room is a study that can also double as a bedroom. Its location makes it especially convenient for weekend guests. If you like this floor plan, there is a range of exterior styles from which to choose. The first is distinctly Tudor; the second traditional, with such details as shutters and multipaned windows; the third is clean and contemporary. Whatever you choose, one exterior element remains constant to complement any of these plans: an irregularly shaped rear terrace that encourages natural growth.

A raised hearth is the centerpiece of the living room, visible also from the dining area. Ceiling beams and paneled walls add to this space's comfortable feeling.

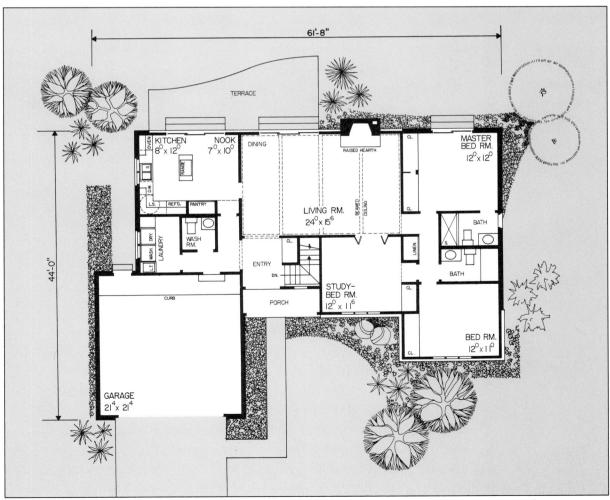

Single floor:
1,584 square feet

 he traditional Tudor exterior of this house disguises a floor plan that provides an abundance of cozy spaces and private views. Located off the master bedroom is a small terrace, an extension of the terrace that runs across the rear of the entire house. A study adjacent to the gathering room could also double as a guest bedroom, especially since there is a bathroom conveniently down the hall. From the sun porch, gathering room, and dining room at the rear of the house there is access to the terrace by way of sliding glass doors. Views of yet another terrace, on the side of the house, can be enjoyed from the breakfast room, which features a built-in desk.

A stenciled pattern above sliding doors in the study adds a warm, personal touch to this space. The doors lead to a rear sun porch.

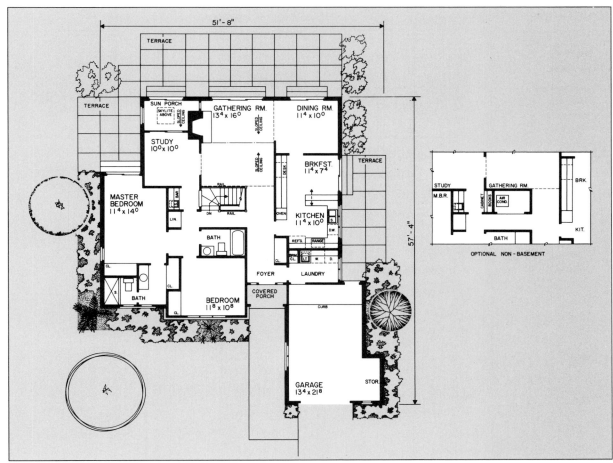

51'-8"

TERRACE

TERRACE

SUN PORCH
SKYLITE ABOVE
SLOPED CEILING

GATHERING RM.
13⁴ x 16⁰
SLOPED CEILING

DINING RM.
11⁴ x 10⁰

STUDY
10⁰ x 10⁰

DESK

BRKFST.
11⁴ x 7⁴

TERRACE

MASTER
BEDROOM
11⁴ x 14⁰

RAIL
DN   RAIL

LIN.

OVEN

KITCHEN
11⁴ x 10⁰

D.W.

BATH

REF'D.   RANGE

CL.

BATH

CL.

BEDROOM
11⁸ x 10⁸

FOYER

LAUNDRY

W   D

COVERED
PORCH

CURB

GARAGE
13⁴ x 21⁸

STOR.

57'-4"

OPTIONAL NON-BASEMENT

STUDY

M.B.R.

GATHERING RM.

CABINET   BOOKS

AIR COND.

BRK.

BATH

KIT.

Single floor:

1,584 square feet

ere a large combination living room-dining room with a sloped ceiling looks out over an old-fashioned covered porch, accessible through sliding glass doors. This porch has been updated distinctively with a trio of skylights. In a space larger than the dining room there is a breakfast room, separated from the kitchen by a snack bar. Nearby is a built-in desk, ideal for preparing shopping lists or paying bills. The traditional kitchen work triangle is reinforced by the placement of a pantry nearby for storage. Setting the master bedroom at a corner of the house allows it to have an expanse of windows on two walls, letting light flood the space. The most central of the house's three bedrooms features double entryways. One, just off the foyer, makes this room ideal for television-watching or study. The other entryway, off a hallway near the bath, is convenient when the space is used as a guest bedroom.

From the breakfast room there is a view to the covered porch, which is perfect for brunches or relaxing on summer evenings.

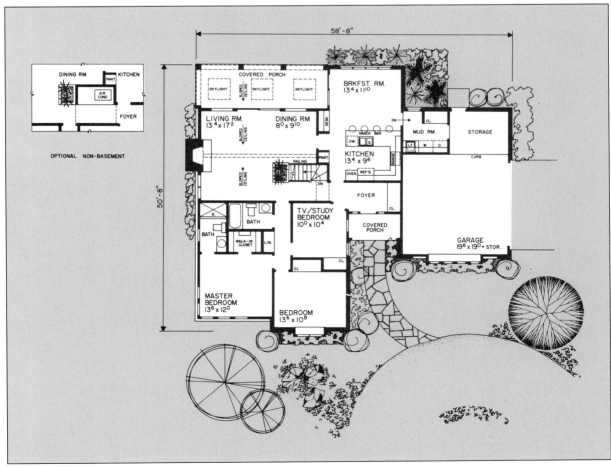

Single floor:
1,729 square feet

For the family that enjoys entertaining, this spacious floor plan provides a variety of areas for both formal and informal occasions. The large gathering room, with its sloped ceiling and fireplace, is located immediately off the foyer. From here guests can move directly into the dining room for either buffet or sit-down dinners. The covered dining porch nearby is perfect for after-dinner drinks and coffee. The cook's job is made easy, because the kitchen is located close to all three areas. With this floor plan, the family can enjoy a particularly large breakfast room almost equal in size to the dining room. There is no shortage of storage space in this plan, as can be seen in the area located off the garage. An optional plan, without a basement, is also provided.

A window seat in the front bedroom provides a tranquil spot for reading or just relaxing.

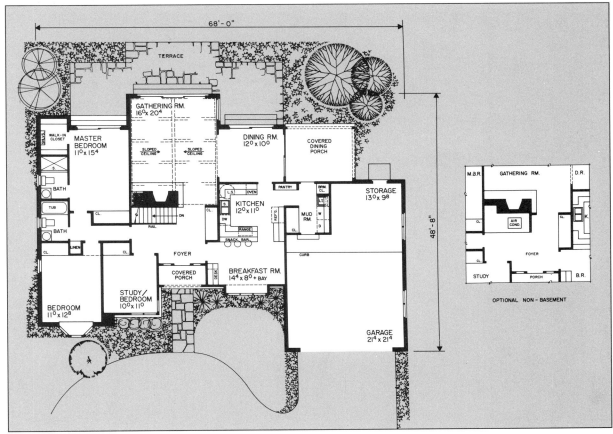

68'-0"

48'-8"

TERRACE

GATHERING RM.
16⁰ x 20⁴

DINING RM.
12⁰ x 10⁰

COVERED DINING PORCH

WALK-IN CLOSET

MASTER BEDROOM
11⁰ x 15⁴

SLOPED CEILING

SLOPED CEILING

BATH

TUB

BATH

KITCHEN
12⁰ x 11⁰

PANTRY

STORAGE
13⁰ x 9⁸

MUD RM.

RANGE

SNACK BAR.

LINEN

FOYER

BREAKFAST RM.
14⁴ x 8⁰ + BAY

CURB

STUDY/ BEDROOM
10⁰ x 11⁰

COVERED PORCH

BEDROOM
11⁰ x 12⁸

GARAGE
21⁴ x 21⁴

M.B.R.

GATHERING RM.

D.R.

AIR COND.

K.

STUDY

PORCH

B.R.

FOYER

OPTIONAL NON-BASEMENT

Single floor:
1,769 square feet

his floor plan offers the option of a basement reached by stairs off a back hallway, but whether or not a basement is a requirement, this plan is certain to meet the needs of an active family. A total of three walk-in closets off the bedrooms provide ample storage. A bathroom next to the dining room is especially convenient for guests. The living room, with its beamed ceiling and raised fireplace, is certain to compete with the family room for popularity. A snack bar between the kitchen and family room lends a sense of informality to mealtime.

In the living room, mixed textures, such as stone for the raised fireplace and wood paneling on the walls, add a feeling of country warmth.

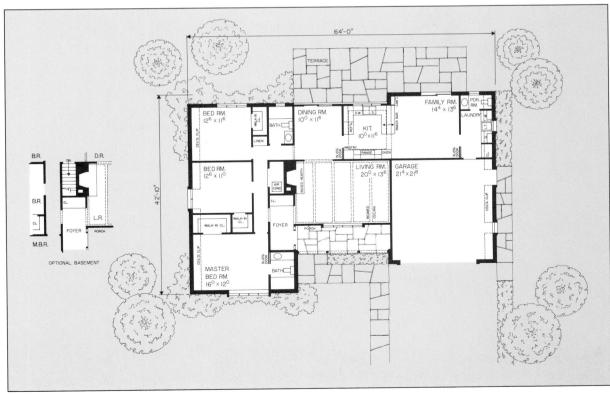

Single floor:

1,646 square feet

 gracious curved driveway in front of this house may remind prospective homeowners of rural English country houses. The windows with diamond-shaped panes also lend a common Tudor-style touch. Another design element is the traditional mudroom, an area rapidly gaining popularity again after going out of fashion years ago in American houses. What better location for it than off the garage and adjacent to the kitchen? An ample entrance court leads visitors inside, through an entry hall and directly into the living room, located this time in the rear of the house, overlooking the terrace. The placement of this room allows it to interact with the adjacent family room and terrace to provide a spacious entertaining area. The family will find the living room practical because of its proximity to the kitchen.

Raised-panel
kitchen cabinetry
with a pass-through
underneath acts as a
room divider and
complements the
traditional style of
the family room.

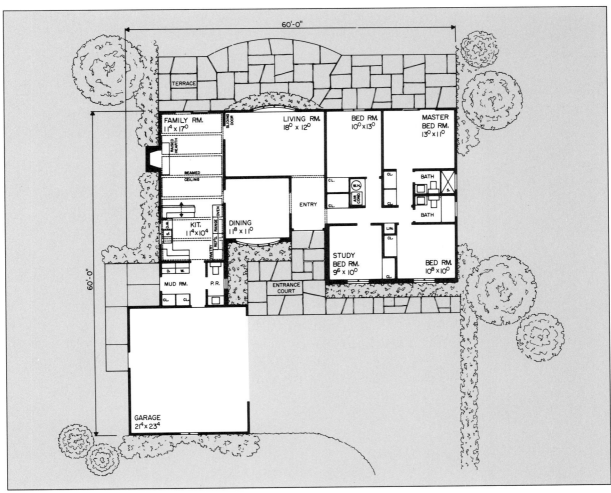

Single floor:

1,796 square feet

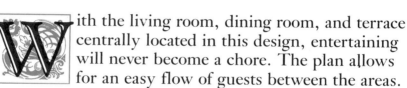ith the living room, dining room, and terrace centrally located in this design, entertaining will never become a chore. The plan allows for an easy flow of guests between the areas. For the family's convenience and privacy, bedrooms are located away from heavy traffic. Storage is an important consideration throughout this house, but especially in the master bedroom. It has double closets as well as a large walk-in closet. A linen closet is convenient to the bedrooms, and at the entry there is another closet. The breakfast nook features its own pantry, and the laundry room plan allows for a closet and extra storage space. A washroom is also conveniently located here, for use by children on their way in from play or school.

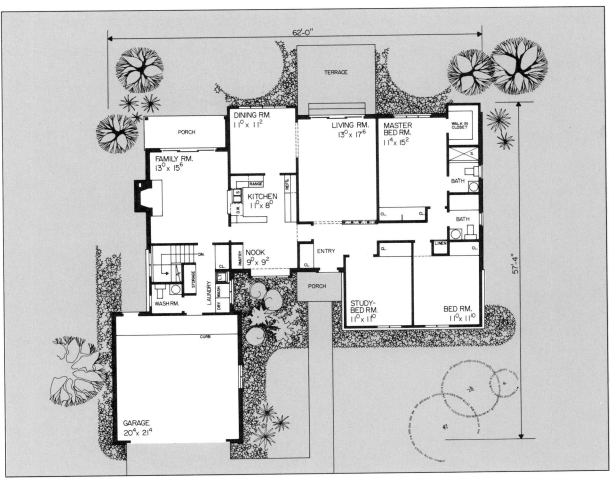

Turned spindles above a half-wall bring a feeling of openness to the entry hall, located adjacent to the living room. The door at right leads to a breakfast nook.

Single floor:
1,825 square feet

an a kitchen be more ideally located than this one? Placed between the combination living-dining room and the family room, it makes serving meals, whether formal or informal, a relatively easy task. Although practicality is important in this design, aesthetics have not been ignored: This is a house planned with views in mind. For instance, from the entrance to the living room there is a view to both the fireplace and the terrace beyond the dining room's sliding glass doors. Adjacent to the master bedroom is a bath and dressing room that includes a large walk-in closet. Another bath, located off a side hallway, serves the other two bedrooms.

A cushioned window seat provides extra seating in the master bedroom, where there is enough space to accommodate a casual grouping of chairs around a coffee table.

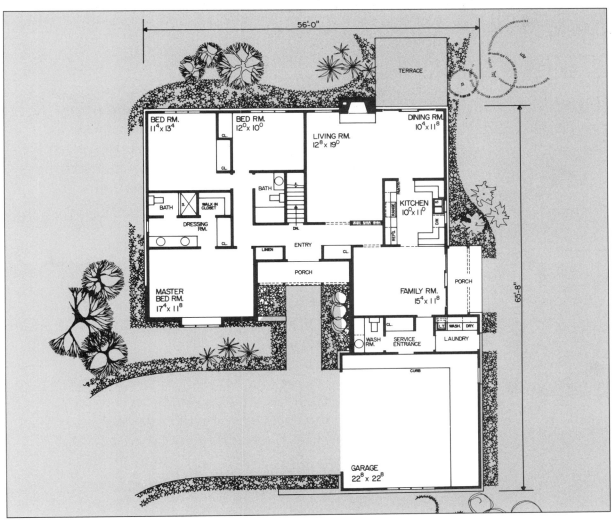

Single floor:
1,956 square feet

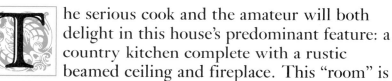

The serious cook and the amateur will both delight in this house's predominant feature: a country kitchen complete with a rustic beamed ceiling and fireplace. This "room" is actually two separate spaces—a kitchen at one end and an area for relaxation at the other—united by a central counter or work island. Homeowners and guests alike will delight in this arrangement, which encourages visitors to participate in meal preparation. The cook can thus continue working while enjoying conversation with guests. For more formal occasions, the hosts and their guests can move to the adjacent dining room. In this design the living room is replaced with a traditional keeping room, featuring its own fireplace and sliding glass doors leading to the rear terrace. This area runs almost the full width of the structure and is accessible also from the country kitchen. For greater privacy, all three bedrooms are located away from these centers of activity. This design offers an optional basement plan.

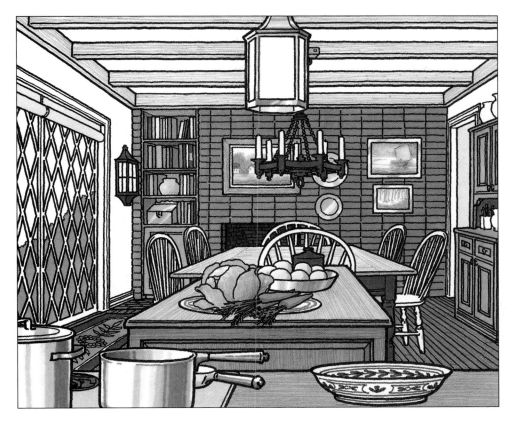

From the island in the country kitchen is a view across the room to the far wall, which has a fireplace and built-in bookshelves. This counter doubles as a space for preparing food and for eating snacks.

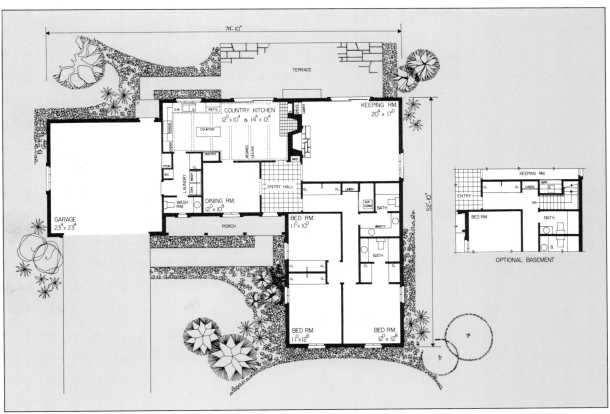

Single floor:
1,919 square feet

irst impressions are important; the entrance to this house makes a gracious one. On either side of the walkway are beds for plantings. The walk area is partially concealed from the street by a low brick wall that runs from the driveway to the front corner of the house. A view of the stone walkway and the foliage bordering it can be enjoyed by family and guests from either the living room or dining room. In effect, the design furnishes a trio of vertical living spaces: a bedroom area, a living and family room area, and a kitchen-dining room area. In the rear of the house, the stone pattern of the front walkway is repeated on a large terrace accessible from either the master bedroom or family room.

In the dining room, a recessed window with diamond-shaped panes in the Tudor style overlooks the front courtyard.

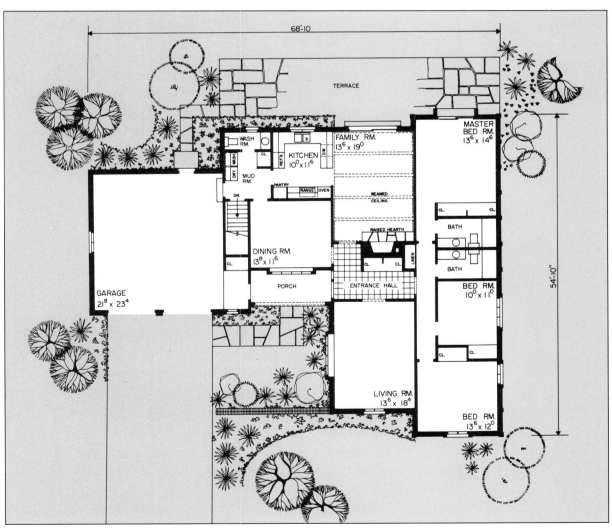

First floor:
1,078 square feet
Second floor:
880 square feet

This floor plan can accommodate a range of architectural styles. The distinctly Tudor architectural elements of the first style shown, including decorative half-timbering and windowpanes in diamond shapes, more than meet the needs of enthusiasts of this style. If your preference is for a traditional look, the second style offers a slightly modified design featuring a gently sloping roof, multi-paned windows, and a front door with sidelights and raised panels. The third elevation shown honors a style from another time and place, with decorative wrought iron in the form of columns and a balcony reminiscent of nineteenth-century New Orleans. Inside, in all three plans, homeowners can enjoy up-to-date convenience with a family room easily accessible from the kitchen. A terrace running the width of the house is perfect for entertaining.

A built-in cabinet and bookshelves not only act as a divider between the family room and breakfast nook, but also provide added storage space.

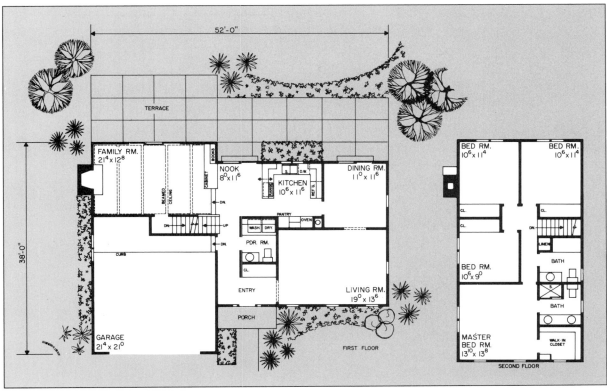

TERRACE

52'-0"

38'-0"

FAMILY RM.
21⁴ x 12⁸

BEAMED CEILING

CABINET

BOOKS

NOOK
8⁰ x 11⁶

KITCHEN
10⁶ x 11⁶

RANGE

S   D.W

REF G.

DINING RM.
11⁰ x 11⁶

DN.

DN.

UP

PANTRY

WASH.   DRY.

OVEN

PDR. RM.

CL.

ENTRY

LIVING RM.
19⁰ x 13⁶

CURB

PORCH

GARAGE
21⁴ x 21⁰

FIRST FLOOR

BED RM.
10⁶ x 11⁴

BED RM.
10⁶ x 11⁴

CL.

CL.

CL.

DN.

LINEN

BATH

BED RM.
10⁶ x 9⁰

S

BATH

MASTER
BED RM.
13¹⁰ x 13⁸

WALK-IN
CLOSET

SECOND FLOOR

Single floor:

1,971 square feet

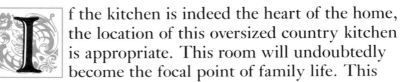

If the kitchen is indeed the heart of the home, the location of this oversized country kitchen is appropriate. This room will undoubtedly become the focal point of family life. This space offers options for a variety of activities: eating, entertaining, reading, and relaxing. Its centerpiece is the fireplace, with its raised hearth. Also contributing to the warm ambience are floor-to-ceiling bookshelves, a built-in desk, paneled walls, and ceiling beams. For the cook there is a central island offering a variety of functions, including a built-in range for cooking and space both for preparing food and for having a quick snack. There is a separate living room and dining room for more formal occasions. The latter features yet another built-in, this time a china cabinet. Both rooms provide views of the terrace. For the convenience of guests, there is a powder room nearby. Even the garage has several added features, such as a large storage area and a workbench.

From the eating area of the country kitchen there is a view to the room's conversation area, which is complete with built-in book-shelves and a desk.

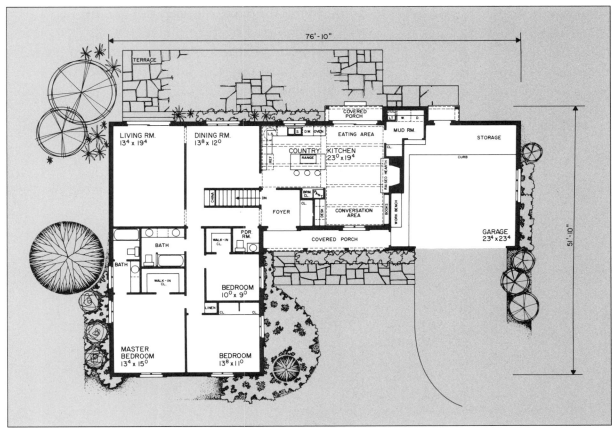

Main level:
795 square feet
Upper level:
912 square feet
Lower level:
335 square feet

 Three levels for living are incorporated into the design of this suburban Tudor. The lower level includes a double-car garage, family room, laundry room, and powder room. On the next level are the living room, dining room, kitchen, and breakfast area. Upstairs is reserved almost exclusively for sleeping, although one bedroom can double as a study. The master bedroom features not only a dressing room and walk-in closet but also its own balcony, located above the terrace with a view toward the rear garden. Adjacent to this wing of the house is a wealth of storage space.

A raised breakfast area overlooks the family room; the railing serves to define the spaces further.

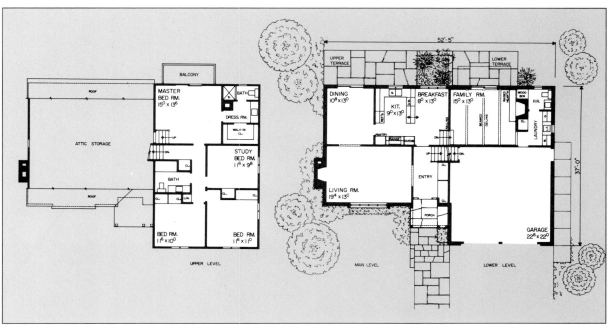

Single floor:
2,029 square feet

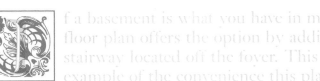

If a basement is what you have in mind, this floor plan offers the option by adding a stairway located off the foyer. This is just one example of the convenience this plan provides, packaged in the most traditional looking of houses. Outside details such as the large central chimney combine with half-timbering to help complete the Tudor look. Inside, serving food is made easier by the location of a snack counter that separates the kitchen from the family room. The master bedroom offers its own private view of the terrace.

Turned spindles help to define both living and dining rooms, yet don't interfere with the four-unit casement windows in either room.

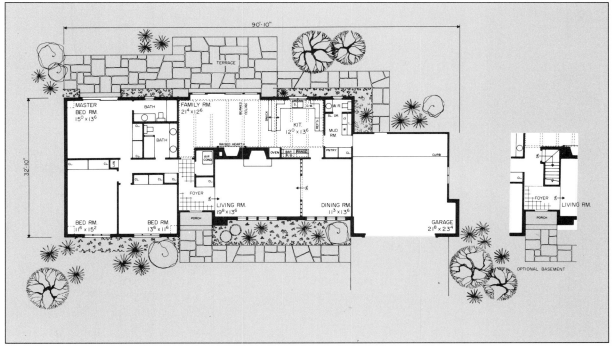

First floor:
1,152 square feet
Second floor:
896 square feet

ack of storage space, a common problem facing most homeowners today, is solved admirably by the floor plan of this house. A second-floor storage area runs the full length of the area above the garage and family room, providing ample overflow space for belongings that still won't fit into the many closets already incorporated into the second story. In fact, this house demonstrates practicality in a variety of forms. On the first floor, visitors can move from entry to living room and dining room, then on to the spacious terrace, allowing food preparation in the kitchen to continue undisturbed. The plan also works for family members, but somewhat in reverse: The proximity of the kitchen and breakfast room to the family room encourages interaction while eating and relaxing. Having access to the terrace through sliding-glass doors extends the amount of space available for conviviality.

A floral motif on floor tiles, stairway, and walls at the entry serves as a unifying element.

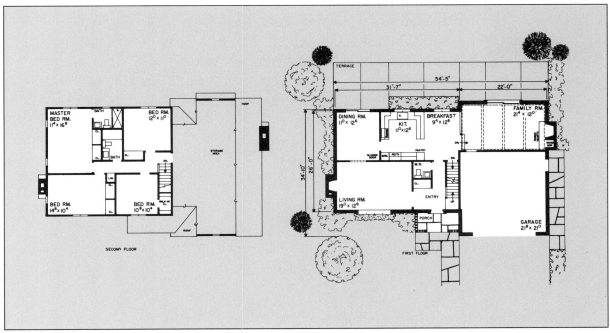

Single floor:
2,057 square feet

etails typical of the Tudor style are evident in this late twentieth-century update. Among them are decorative half-timbering, a stone entryway, and a large, prominently located chimney. Window groupings across the front of the house honor the Tudor design but also guarantee sun-filled rooms. Inside, however, the floor plan is designed to meet contemporary needs. The unloading of groceries and other household items is made easier by the placement of a door off the garage that leads to the laundry room and kitchen. The master bedroom provides the ultimate in convenience and privacy with its large walk-in closet and accessibility to a part of the rear terrace. This is a terrace the whole family can enjoy, however, from a sliding glass door off the family room.

A two-part divider between living room and dining room gives both areas a sense of spaciousness.

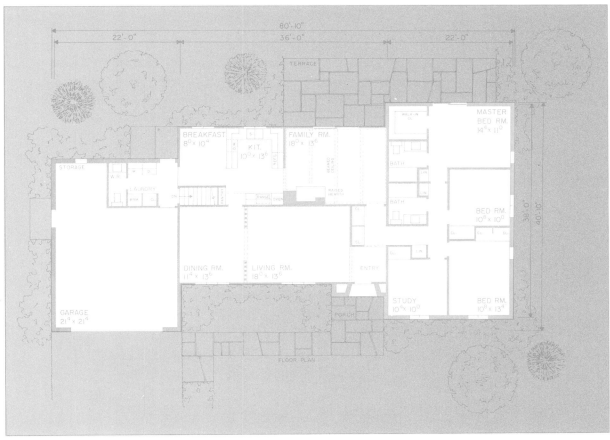

Single floor:
2,132 square feet

 lean, contemporary lines combine here with traditional Tudor elements such as decorative half-timbering, diamond-shaped window panes, and large chimneys to create a distinctive form. The result is akin to a ranch house with Tudor details. The floor plan enhances the views from inside to out that are available from every room in the rear of the house: family room, nook, dining room, living room, and even the master bedroom. And, with the exception only of the nook, each room has sliding glass doors to provide access to the terrace. The bedroom arrangement encourages privacy, especially with the placement of one bedroom away from the rest. This layout makes that bedroom an ideal guest room or, if the homeowners prefer, a library or study. Two other bedrooms are linked by a bath and double vanity, perfect for sharing by the children of the house.

From the family room, a window provides a view of one section of the rear terrace. The informal arrangement of furniture around the fireplace encourages conversation.

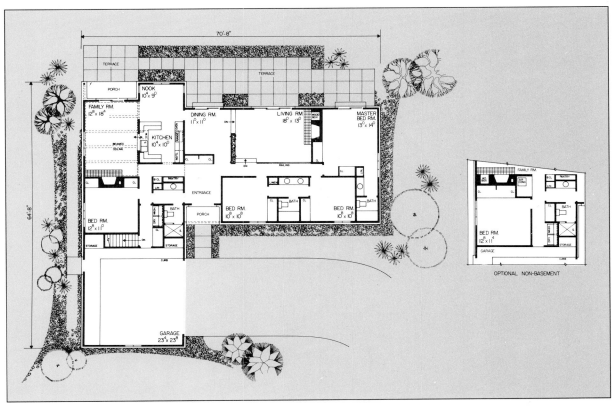

First floor:

2,112 square feet

The compact design of this one-story house nevertheless presents a variety of features often associated with much larger structures. Here the gathering room and dining room merge into one space made even more comfortable by a fireplace. The kitchen has not only an island but also a built-in pantry and a broom closet. Adjacent to it is the breakfast room which, like the other rooms in the rear of the house, provides access to a spacious terrace. In the master suite there is a large walk-in closet and a pair of vanity sinks for added convenience. The study, located away from the major traffic areas of the house, might well double as a guest bedroom. The facade's traditional Tudor detailing includes decorative half-timbering, cross-gables, and multipaned windows.

Generous windows create a cozy corner, perfect for quiet reading and relaxing, that affords a generous view of the entrance courtyard.

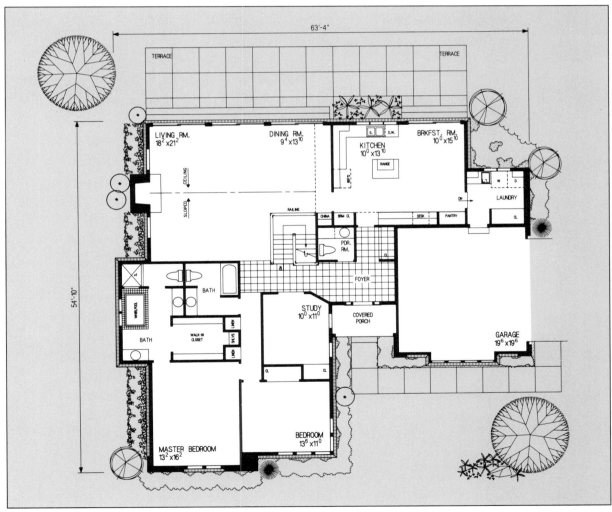

First floor:
1,327 square feet
Second floor:
832 square feet

 pleasing balance is achieved in the facade of this home. Central to the design is a typical Tudor architectural element: a front-facing gable with decorative half-timbers. One "wing" of the house is actually a two-car garage. Off this space is the mudroom, a practical feature common in early English and American homes that is now coming back into vogue. Visitors enter the house along a path to a porch floored with slate that extends in to the entry hall. More formal entertaining is reserved for this front half of the house, with its large living room. Dinner guests can move directly across the foyer to the dining room. How many homes can boast of a living room, family room, and terrace—all approximately the same size? Built-in bookshelves on either side of the fireplace in the family room make this area especially inviting. The second floor boasts plenty of closet space, including a walk-in version off the master bedroom and a linen closet at the top of the stairs.

An elegant mural depicting a wooded scene—perhaps one visible from this very house—sets the tone for an entry hall where textures such as slate and wood mix comfortably.

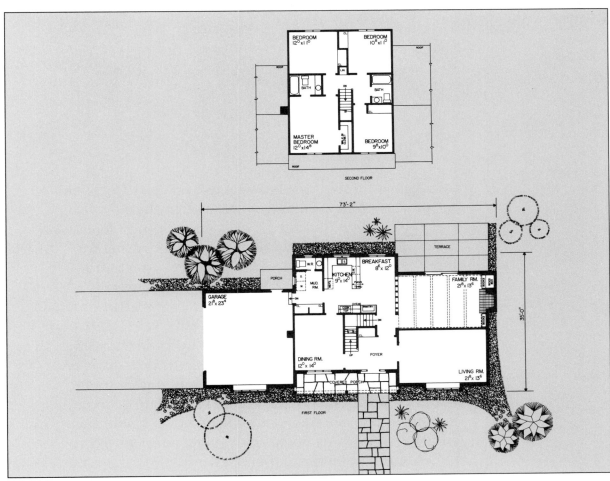

First floor:
1,309 square feet
Second floor:
860 square feet

 You don't have to move to England's Cotswolds to enjoy cottage living, as this charming design illustrates. This stone cottage looks as though it could have been in its setting for more than a century, but what appears to be a more recently added wing (*far right*, *street view*) is actually a two-car garage. The integrity of the design carries through whether the house is viewed from the street or the garden. The family can move easily from the garage into the kitchen and family room without ever disturbing people in the formal living room and dining room. On either side of the raised hearth in the family room are built-in bookshelves. And what cottage would be complete without its nook? This nook, adjacent to the kitchen, provides a quiet spot for reading.

Traditional furnishings complement the cottage atmosphere in this home. Instead of a window seat in the living room, the designers have used a wooden bench, complemented by the addition of paneled doors beneath built-in bookshelves.

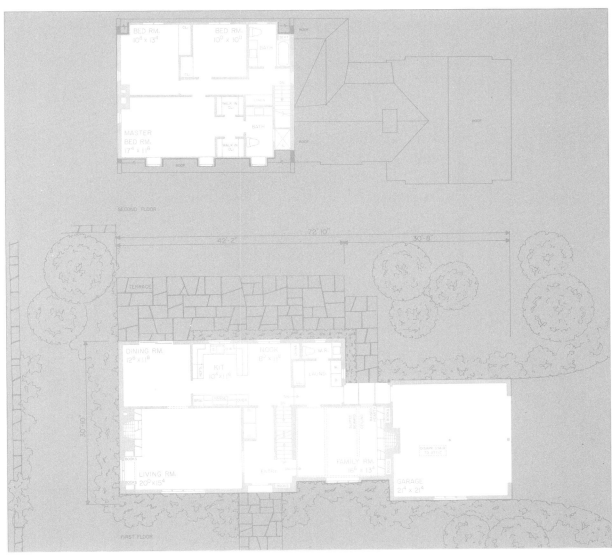

Single floor:

2,282 square feet

This cottage's private and public spaces extend to outside areas. Off the master bedroom is a "quiet" terrace, perfect for enjoying early morning coffee and the newspaper or relaxing at the end of a long day. Just outside the family room is a larger "living" terrace, where the whole family can dine in the summer months. Its spaciousness and proximity to the family room make this terrace ideal for informal entertaining. Practicality is also a key part of this design, with its double closets and wall of cabinets in the dressing room off the master bedroom. In the garage, a large space to the rear provides extra storage for the lawn mower and garden tools.

In the family room, adjacent to the kitchen, a fireplace helps divide the two spaces.

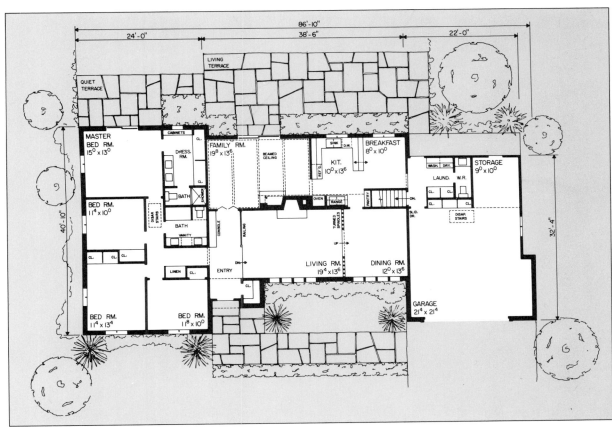

First floor:
1,261 square feet

Second floor:
950 square feet

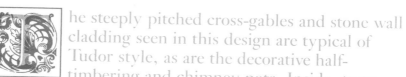

The steeply pitched cross-gables and stone wall cladding seen in this design are typical of Tudor style, as are the decorative half-timbering and chimney pots. Inside, twentieth-century convenience is a priority. Casual meals can be prepared and served at the snack bar dividing the kitchen from the family room. A formal terrace located in the rear of the house is accessible from several rooms. The stone applied on the facade is also used on the rear terrace. A covered porch off the family room is the ideal location for a late breakfast or for informal entertaining. The second floor comfortably accommodates a master suite with dressing room, two other bedrooms, and a room that can be used as a nursery, lounge, or study.

The hooded living room fireplace is a striking architectural element that accommodates a casual grouping of furniture.

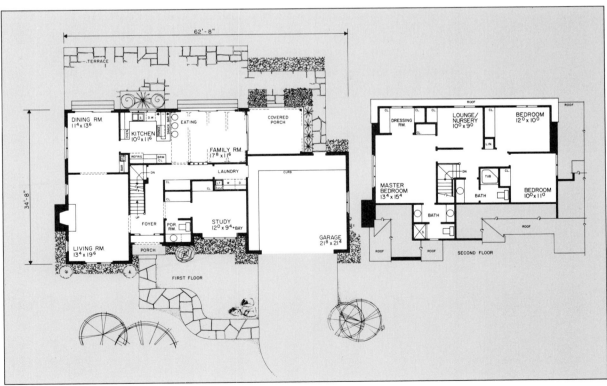

First floor:
1,160 square feet
Second floor:
1,222 square feet

 omeowners with large families will find that this design more than adequately meets their needs, yet the exterior details still celebrate the Tudor style. Upstairs there are five bedrooms, including a master suite with dressing room, a double-sink vanity, and a large walk-in closet. Another full bathroom serves the other bedrooms. Lots of closet space, including two linen closets, is allowed for in the upstairs plan. Downstairs it's likely that the family room will become the activity center of the home. Here a snack bar is located adjacent to the kitchen to encourage informal meals and family gatherings.

What better place to relax than in this family room, with its brick fireplace, built-in bookshelves, and beamed ceiling. Glass doors provide direct access to the terrace.

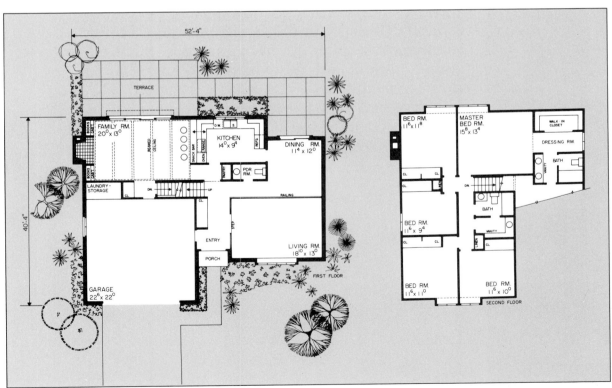

First floor:

1,262 square feet

Second floor:

1,108 square feet

y placing the kitchen between the breakfast and dining rooms, this plan makes life easier for the cook. Because food preparation is largely confined within the U-shaped kitchen, family members and guests can move from either the breakfast or the dining room into the nearby family room without disturbing the cook. Sliding glass doors lead from both the family and dining rooms to a terrace extending across the back of the house. The house's second story features a powder room conveniently located at the top of the stairs for guests, as well as a sewing area, which could easily double as a space for reading and relaxing or as a guest room.

A sunny alcove in a second-floor corner bedroom has enough space to accommodate a desk.

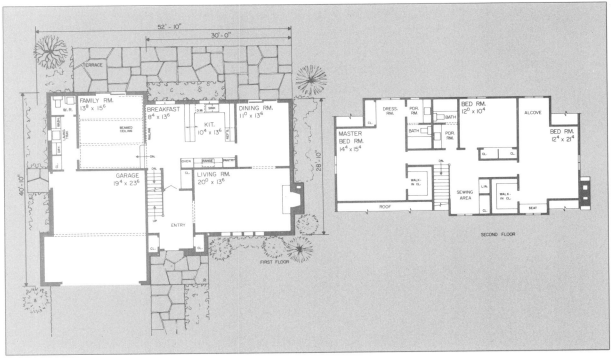

First floor:
1,804 square feet
Second floor:
939 square feet

How many houses can boast of their own lounge? This one is a part of the upstairs master suite. Offering the ultimate in privacy and convenience, the master suite also features a trio of walk-in closets and even a separate dressing area. Any storage overflow can conveniently be placed in the spacious storage areas on the same level. Downstairs, double entry doors lead visitors into a large hallway, from which they can proceed either into the living room or directly into the dining room. A terrace, accessible from both rooms through sliding doors, extends the entertainment space. A mudroom off the garage encourages everyone entering to deposit outdoor clothing and wipe their shoes.

With a fireplace as its centerpiece, this intimate lounge off the master suite upstairs features a sloped ceiling that adds architectural interest to the room.

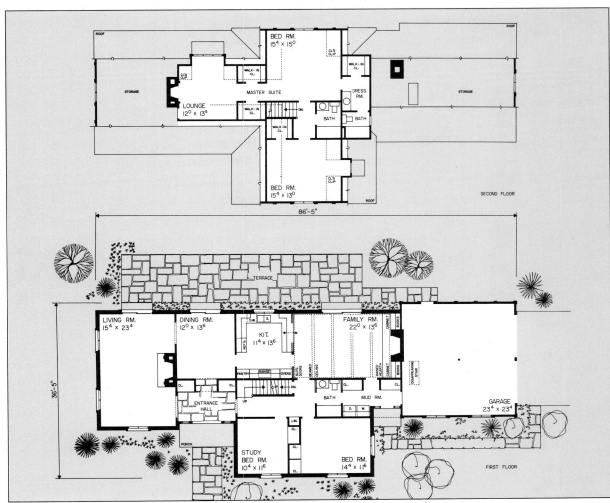

Main level:

936 square feet

Upper level:

971 square feet

Lower level:

971 square feet

t the very center of this home is its entrance hall, featuring a graceful staircase. From here guests can enter either the living room, with its comfortable fireplace and built-in bookshelves, or the dining room. For the homeowners, entrance to the house is easiest from the garage, from which they have access to a mudroom before entering the kitchen. Here a nook big enough to accommodate a table and chairs is the perfect spot for family breakfasts. Upstairs, where the master suite and two other bedrooms are located, a hallway encourages privacy. Below this area is yet another level, equal in size to the upstairs bedroom space. Although the family room, which has a raised hearth and beamed ceiling, is central to this space, there is also an extra bedroom (perfect for weekend guests), a laundry room, and even a room for hobbyists.

The entryway faces a staircase that provides access to both upper and lower levels of the house and also overlooks the living room.

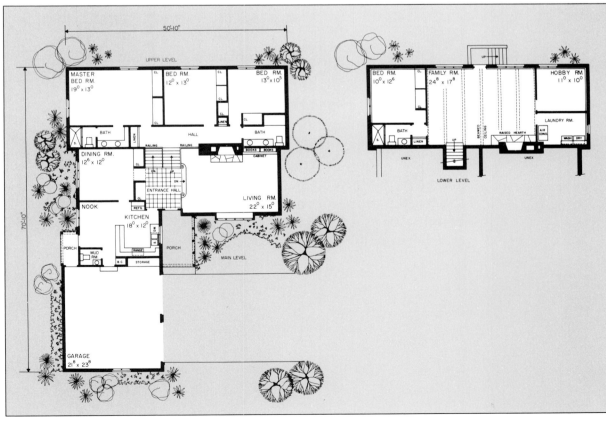

Main level:
987 square feet

Upper level:
1,043 square feet

Lower level:
463 square feet

rom the street, this appears to be the most conventional of houses, thanks to the prominence of its Tudor detailing, including unusually tall half-timbering on the facade. What this house's gently sloping lawn helps disguise, however, is a roomy floor plan made possible by a lower level that has a garage, a family room, a washroom, and a laundry room. A wing of bedrooms is set above the garage/family room, each with ample closet space. Off the master bedroom is a large walk-in closet. The floor plan makes entertaining a snap—guests can move with ease between living room, dining room, and terrace.

Leaded wall
sconces above a
raised fireplace add
symmetry to the
mantel area.

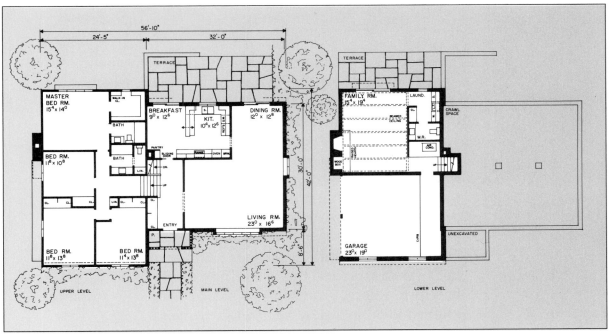

Main level:
1,874 square feet
Lower level:
1,131 square feet

 Tudor style and contemporary convenience merge in this spacious floor plan, which offers amenities rarely found together in one design. A deck extends completely across the rear of the house, overlooking a terrace below. Entertaining guests is convenient with the placement of both the living room and dining room adjacent to the deck. A built-in china cabinet in the breakfast room and a pantry and broom closet in the kitchen ease storage problems. The lower level focuses almost entirely on the family and its needs. It features a combination sauna-hot tub-dressing room and a family room with a raised-hearth fireplace. This house also boasts its own summer kitchen ideal for teenagers and their guests.

A through fire-
place separating the
living room and
dining room can be
enjoyed by the
occupants of
both areas.

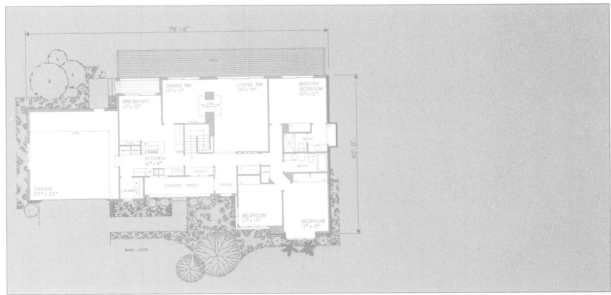

VILLAS

Tudor designs are suited to even the most rustic hideaways or country retreats. Reflecting their environment, Tudor homes feature the natural materials of stone, wood, and brick.

Plan 2855, page 124

 First floor:

991 square feet

Second floor:

952 square feet

or a house with less than 2,000 square feet, this floor plan offers a remarkable diversity of space. Both the living room and dining room are full-sized. There is access to a large rear terrace from the dining room by way of sliding glass doors. The kitchen features a well-placed work triangle and a pantry. The large family room has beamed ceilings, a slate hearth for the fireplace, and a sliding glass door to the terrace. In addition, the first floor offers a foyer, a powder room, and a laundry room. A choice of floor plans is offered for the second floor. The first plan provides four bedrooms plus a master bedroom. The second plan allows for three bedrooms and the master suite, with two of the rear bedrooms being on a larger scale than those in the first plan.

Just off the foyer is the entrance to the conveniently located family room. The door at the right leads to a closet.

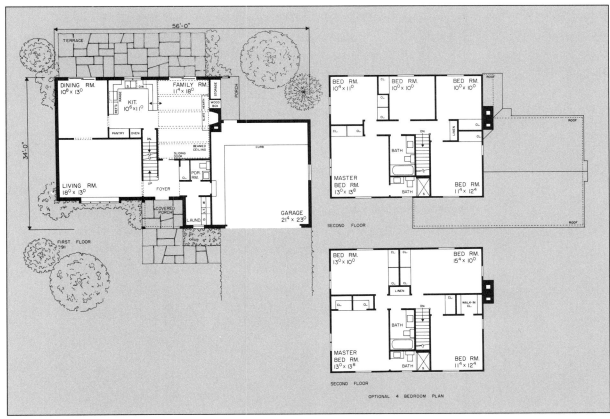

First floor:

999 square feet

Second floor:

997 square feet

 This floor plan makes meals a pleasure to prepare—and serve. The formal dining room and informal breakfast room are both accessible from the kitchen, which separates the two spaces. Whether entertaining friends or simply preparing quick meals for the family, the cook's job is made especially easy. Family and guests will enjoy using the rear terrace. It's simple to walk directly outside through sliding glass doors in the dining room or breakfast room. The family room has been placed next to the breakfast room, an arrangement certain to please homeowners with children. Upstairs, this plan offers an added feature: a nursery/study convenient to the master bedroom. Two other bedrooms are also included.

Window styles mix comfortably in the living room, with casement-style panes in front and diamond-shaped ones on the side.

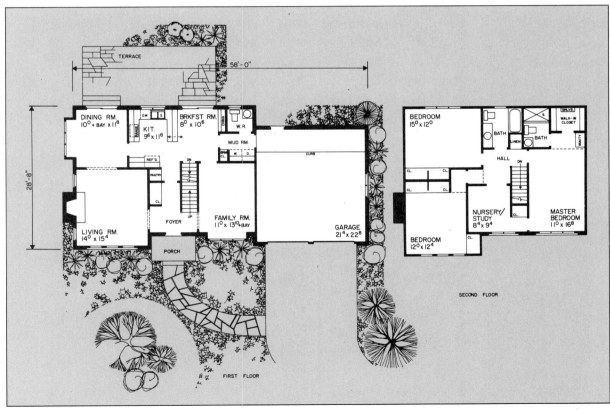

First Floor / Second Floor plan labels:

TERRACE

58' - 0"

28' - 8"

DINING RM.
10⁰ + BAY x 11⁸

KIT.
9⁶ x 11⁸

BRKFST RM.
8⁰ x 10⁶

CHINA

W.R.

MUD RM.

REF'G.

PANTRY

CL.

DN

SPRL

CURB

W D

FOYER

UP

FAMILY RM.
11⁰ x 13¹⁰+BAY

GARAGE
21⁴ x 22⁸

LIVING RM.
14⁰ x 15⁴

PORCH

FIRST FLOOR

BEDROOM
15⁰ x 12⁰

BATH

LINEN

BATH

SHLVS.

WALK-IN
CLOSET

VANITY

HALL

CL.

CL.

CL.

CL.

DN

CL.

NURSERY/
STUDY
8⁴ x 9⁴

MASTER
BEDROOM
11⁰ x 16⁸

BEDROOM
12⁰ x 12⁴

SECOND FLOOR

First floor:

984 square feet

Second floor:

1,003 square feet

his compact plan offers many of the amenities usually found only in larger spaces. Many elements typical of the Tudor style characterize the exterior facade, including diamond-shaped windowpanes, partial stone cladding, and decorative half-timbers, some of them curved. During the warmer months, the large terrace extending across the rear of the house enlarges the floor plan's living space. Formal living room and dining room areas are separate, as is the entry hall. The family room features its own fireplace. On the second floor are four bedrooms with double vanities in the master suite for extra convenience. Both this room and the other bedrooms have plenty of closet space. A separate linen closet is located in the upstairs hallway.

A fireplace with a raised-brick hearth easily becomes the focal point of the family room.

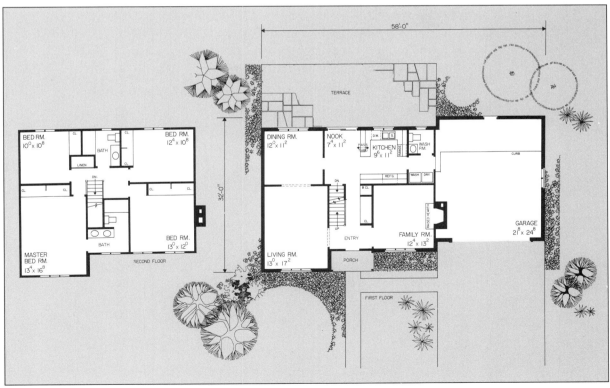

First floor:

1,003 square feet

Second floor:

1,056 square feet

his floor plan offers a multitude of features despite its compactness. With the traditional living room eliminated, the gathering room and dining room adjoin, each space accessible to the rear terrace through its own set of sliding glass doors. A pass-through from kitchen to dining room makes easy the serving of more informal meals. The separate study includes its own large storage area. A mudroom located just off the garage is ideal for storing coats and outerwear. Upstairs, the homeowners can enjoy their own private balcony off the master suite. This suite also includes a dressing room and a walk-in closet with built-in shelving. There are two other bedrooms in this second-floor plan. And while the facade of this house presents the most traditional of Tudor detailing, there is one charming surprise: a window box along the path to the entry.

Occupants of this master bedroom can wake each morning with a restful view of their rear garden.

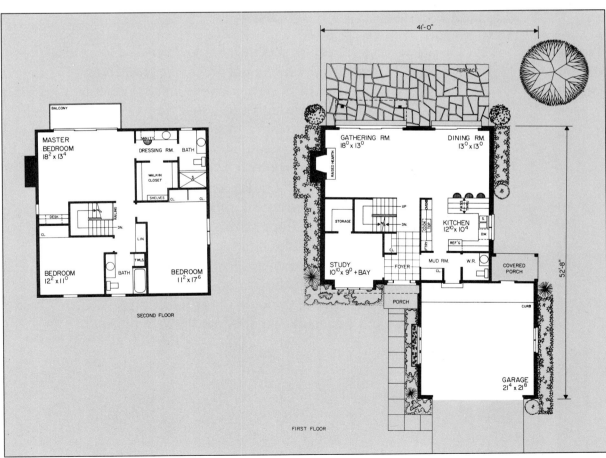

SECOND FLOOR

FIRST FLOOR

First floor:
1,420 square feet

Second floor:
859 square feet

 This facade is accentuated by a trio of dormers giving light to rooms on the second floor. The overall design conveys a sense of continuity, as though the house had been thoughtfully expanded over a period of years. The result is a feeling of permanence and stability. The formal living room and dining room face each other across the entrance hall. Serving is made easy by having the kitchen between the dining room and the more casual eating nook. The first-floor family room is complete with its own wet bar. The nearby study could also double as a guest bedroom, especially as it has a private bath with a shower for added convenience. And adequate storage space is no problem with this plan. Upstairs, each bedroom has its own walk-in closet.

Diamond-shaped windowpanes in the dining room, characteristic of the Tudor style, are repeated in the sidelights of the front door.

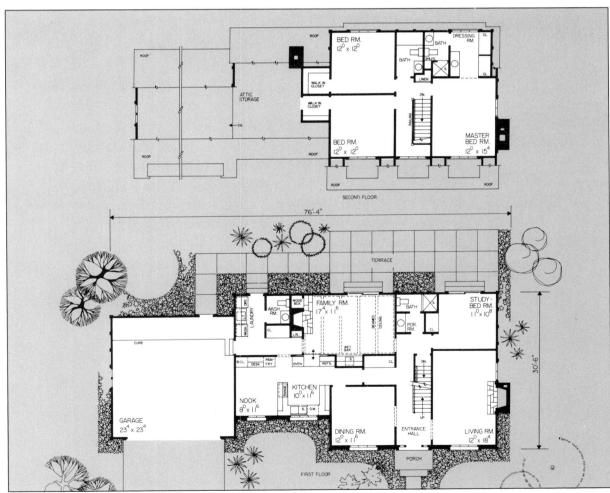

SECOND FLOOR

FIRST FLOOR

76'-4"

30'-6"

First floor:
1,071 square feet

Second floor:
1,022 square feet

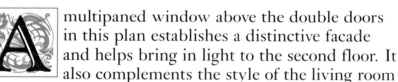

A multipaned window above the double doors in this plan establishes a distinctive facade and helps bring in light to the second floor. It also complements the style of the living room window. Other traditional Tudor-style elements, such as decorative half-timbering and diamond-shaped windowpanes, characterize this plan. The family will undoubtedly spend much of its time in the rear of the house, where the kitchen, family room, and adjoining terrace are located. Beamed ceilings and a fireplace give the family room added ambience and a sense of comfort. The spacious kitchen, with its ideal work triangle, also features a serving counter sure to be a popular gathering place for family and guests. Plenty of closet space has been worked into the upstairs floor plan, with its master suite and two other bedrooms.

A counter separating the kitchen from the family room can function as a buffet when the homeowners entertain.

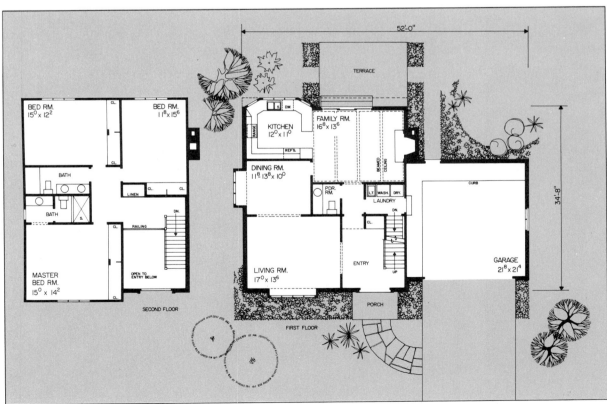

BED RM.
15⁰ x 12²

BED RM.
11⁸ x 15⁶

CL.

CL.

CL.

BATH

CL.

LINEN

CL.

BATH

S.

DN.

CL.

RAILING

OPEN TO
ENTRY BELOW

MASTER
BED RM.
15⁰ x 14²

CL.

SECOND FLOOR

52'-0"

TERRACE

RANGE

S.

DW.

KITCHEN
12⁰ x 11⁰

REF'G.

FAMILY RM.
16⁸ x 13⁶

BEAMED
CEILING

CURB

DINING RM.
11⁸ 13⁸ x 10⁰

PDR.
RM.

LT. WASH. DRY.

LAUNDRY

DN.

CL.

UP

GARAGE
21⁸ x 21⁴

LIVING RM.
17⁰ x 13⁶

ENTRY

PORCH

FIRST FLOOR

34'-8"

First floor:
1,308 square feet
Second floor:
1,063 square feet

Projecting a family room to the rear of the house creates in effect two separate terraces. Sliding glass doors link both areas to the family room. The terrace on the right serves as an extension of the living room to accommodate an overflow of guests. The terrace on the left, located off the breakfast nook, is large enough to accommodate a table and chairs for a perfect place to have a leisurely meal. The family room itself offers a variety of features sure to make it a popular gathering spot: a fireplace with a raised hearth, built-in bookshelves and cabinetry, and a beamed ceiling. A snack bar divides the kitchen from the breakfast nook, to make serving meals quick and easy. Upstairs, there are four bedrooms, including the master suite. A storage area on this floor adds to the plan's convenience.

A staircase with a simple balustrade leads from the first floor to the second.

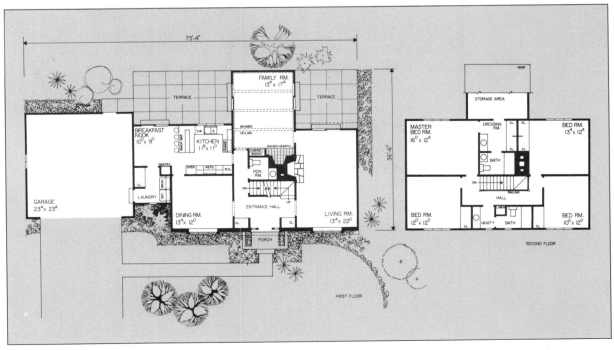

Single level:
2,375 square feet

Gable detailing and casement windows, elements characteristic of Tudor style, are applied to a contemporary ranch form in this plan. The result is a pleasing, balanced facade that provides light-filled interiors. The three-car garage here will be especially beneficial to an active family. A through-fireplace separates living room from family room. Both spaces share views of the main rear terrace. Adjacent to the living room is a sitting room/study that could also double as a home office or library. The master bedroom boasts a private terrace accessible through sliding glass doors. The serious cook will find this kitchen plan ideal: The work triangle is planned for comfortable operation, with the sink set in the island. An extension of the island's surface creates a snack bar.

Serving informal meals is simple with a snack bar built into the kitchen island. The recessed window area is an appealing niche for morning coffee.

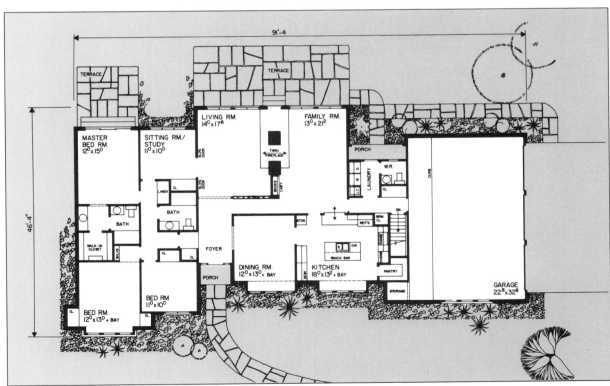

Main level:
904 square feet
Upper level:
1,120 square feet
Lower level:
404 square feet

ecorated verge boards, like those used in the gables of this house, are typical Tudor-style elements, as are the massive central chimney and decorative half-timbering. But in this house plan traditional details combine with contemporary convenience as in the two-car garage. Guests can move easily from the entry hall into either the family room or the living room and dining room without disturbing the cook. During warm weather, two rear terraces on separate levels provide extensions of the homeowners' living space. A beamed ceiling in the family room gives this area a rustic feel, as does the balustrade, distinguishing this space from the eating nook. Upstairs, the master suite's location in the rear of the house affords its occupants a view of the garden. This master suite's large walk-in closet provides more than adequate storage space when combined with the ample closet space in the floor's three other bedrooms.

What better place to enjoy morning coffee than the small balcony off the master bedroom?

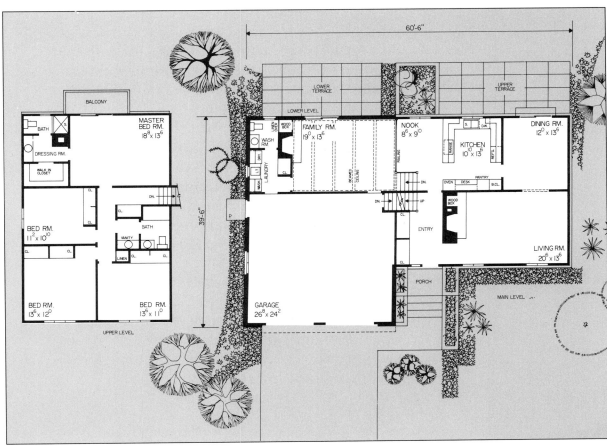

60'-6"

39'-6"

BALCONY

BATH

S

MASTER
BED RM.
18⁸ x 13⁶

DRESSING RM.

WALK-IN
CLOSET

CL

DN.

BED RM.
11² x 10⁰

CL

CL

BATH

CL

CL

VANITY

LINEN
CL
CL

BED RM.
13⁶ x 12⁰

CL

CL

BED RM.
13⁶ x 11⁰

UPPER LEVEL

LOWER TERRACE

UPPER TERRACE

LOWER LEVEL

LINEN
OVEN
WOOD
BOX

FAMILY RM.
19⁰ x 13⁶

NOOK
8⁶ x 9⁰

S.
D.W.

DINING RM.
12⁰ x 13⁶

WASH
RM.

DRY.

WASH

LT.

LAUNDRY

CL

BEAMED
CEILING

RAILING

RANGE

KITCHEN
10⁰ x 13

REF'G.

P

DN.

DN.

UP

OVEN

DESK

PANTRY

B.CL.

WOOD
BOX

CL

ENTRY

LIVING RM.
20⁶ x 13⁶

CL

PORCH

MAIN LEVEL

GARAGE
26⁸ x 24²

Single level:

2,450 square feet

win terraces—one in the rear of the house, another on one side—make this plan attractive. Whether entertaining or simply relaxing with the family is on the agenda, this layout encourages both. The terraces complement the flow of guests and provide more than a single area for entertaining. A vestibule in front of the entry features a closet for hanging coats and hats. A powder room in that hallway adds convenience. The family room extends the full depth of the house from front to rear. Its fireplace, with a raised hearth and a built-in woodbox, are features sure to be appreciated on winter evenings. For the cook, the kitchen has a well-planned work triangle. The adjacent breakfast room includes a pantry and a built-in desk for planning menus, paying bills, and preparing shopping lists. This four-bedroom house includes a master suite with a large walk-in closet.

Exposed beams in the family room add to the rustic character of this space. The window seat affords a view of the front garden.

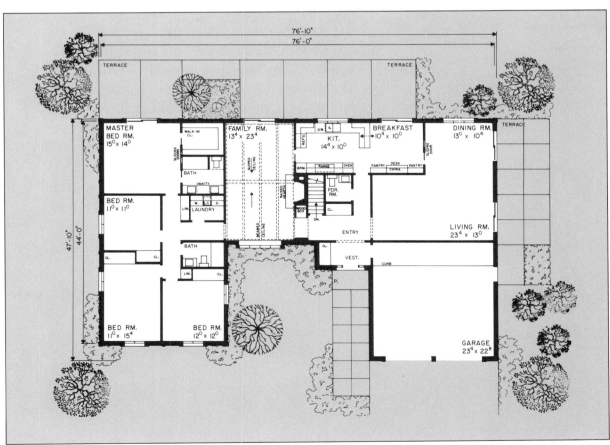

First floor:

1,409 square feet

Second floor:

1,020 square feet

Storage will never be a problem in this house, which has abundant space upstairs and down. One such area, perfect for storing the lawn mower and garden tools, is along the inside wall of the garage. Upstairs there is a permanent staircase from the second floor to the attic, which is certainly able to handle any overflow in storage. The rear of the house is likely to be a popular spot with the homeowners. The family room, breakfast room, and rear terrace flow into one another to work as almost a single space. A built-in desk in the breakfast room provides an appropriate setting for making grocery lists or paying bills. Upstairs are four bedrooms, one of which might double as a study. The master suite's dressing room features double vanities and plenty of closet space.

Ceiling beams and a fireplace with a raised hearth provide rustic touches in the family room.

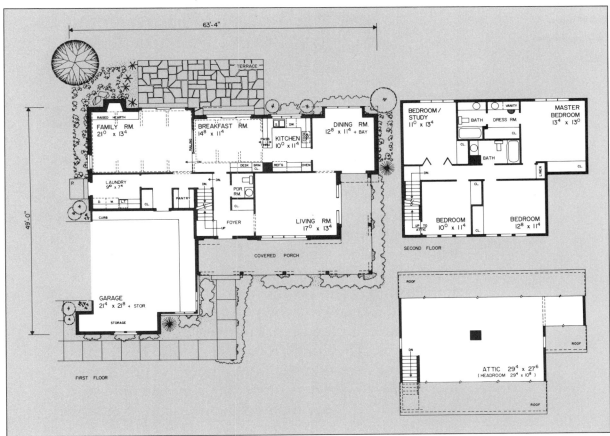

63'-4"

49'-0"

TERRACE

FAMILY RM.
21⁰ x 13⁴
RAISED HEARTH

BREAKFAST RM.
14⁸ x 11⁴

KITCHEN
10⁰ x 11⁴

DINING RM.
12⁸ x 11⁴ + BAY

LAUNDRY
9⁰ x 7⁴

PANTRY

PDR. RM.

FOYER

LIVING RM.
17⁰ x 13⁴

COVERED PORCH

GARAGE
21⁴ x 21⁸ + STOR.

STORAGE

CURB

FIRST FLOOR

BEDROOM /
STUDY
11⁰ x 13⁴

BATH

VANITY

DRESS RM.

MASTER
BEDROOM
13⁴ x 13⁰

BATH

UP TO
ATTIC

BEDROOM
10⁰ x 11⁴

BEDROOM
12⁸ x 11⁴

LINEN

SECOND FLOOR

ROOF

ROOF

ATTIC 29⁴ x 27⁶
(HEADROOM 29⁴ x 10⁸)

ROOF

First floor:
1,256 square feet
Second floor:
1,351 square feet

The ambience of a rustic hideaway is conveyed by the facade of this house. Introducing a meandering walkway to the entrance and employing natural landscaping would accentuate this feeling. The conventional Tudor detailing of diamond-shaped windowpanes and huge chimneys seems less formal than usual in this design because simple shutters and porch columns help offset the traditional formality of the style. An extra-large living room features a raised-hearth fireplace and built-in bookshelves. The family room, which also has a raised hearth, looks out over the front garden. On the second floor are four bedrooms, including a master suite with two separate dressing rooms. One bedroom has its own walk-in closet.

Double doors greet visitors to this home. Once inside, guests can walk directly into the large living room, set off from the hallway by a balustrade.

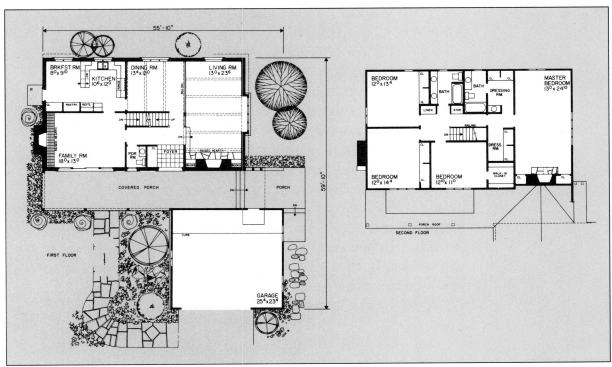

First floor:

1,566 square feet

Second floor:

930 square feet

here's little doubt that the family room in this plan, centrally located in the design, will become the focal point of activity in the house. This room features a fireplace and sloped ceilings. Easy access to the garden is provided through a pair of sliding glass doors. This space, adjacent to the dining room and kitchen, is ideal also for entertaining. A second fireplace, with its own woodbox, is located in the living room. The single first-floor bedroom can have a variety of uses as a child's room, guest bedroom, or private study. Upstairs, three bedrooms are provided in this plan. The master suite features ample closet space and both a dressing room and a walk-in closet. The exterior features strong Tudor architectural details such as decorative half-timbering, a steeply pitched roof, and tall windows. Two large chimneys, both with decorative chimney pots, are another hallmark of Tudor style.

Recessed French doors in the dining room lead to a rear terrace and add to the room's sense of spaciousness.

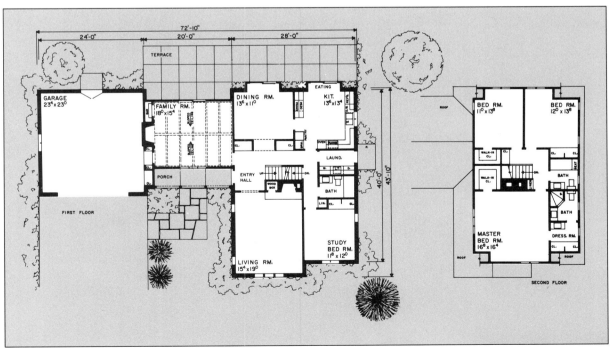

First floor:
1,372 square feet
Second floor:
1,245 square feet

ormal and gracious, but with a floor plan to meet today's needs, this house excels in all respects. Central to the downstairs layout is a large family room with a fireplace. Beyond this is a covered porch perfect in warmer months for family barbecues and informal entertaining. The terrace below is partly covered by the porch but extends beyond it and is accessible from the breakfast room. A special feature of this plan is a large storage area adjoining the garage. With the addition of a simple partition, this space might easily be converted to a hobby or sewing room. A spacious dressing room is part of the master suite on the second floor. A window seat in this room is an added touch of comfort that makes the space distinctive.

124

A recessed window in the dining room creates space for plants, giving the room a solariumlike effect. Wainscoting divides the wall space for a formal touch.

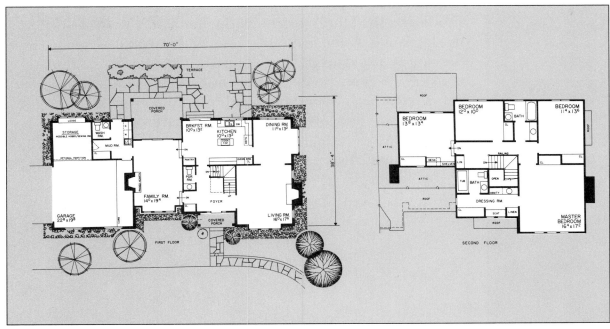

First floor:
1,555 square feet
Second floor:
1,080 square feet

This house's facade is distinguished by an architectural element characteristic of the Tudor style. The oriel, or projecting bay window (supported here by brackets), dominates the gable. The floor plan provides a direct view of the dining room from the entrance hall. This plan features two fireplaces, one in the living room and another in the family room. In the kitchen, a perfect work triangle helps make any cook's job much easier. Serving is also convenient because of the adjacent eating nook. A spacious porch, accessible through sliding glass doors from both living room and dining room, is a welcome addition. Another attractive feature is the large walk-in closet on the first floor. There is additional storage in the attic.

Built-in shelves and a cabinet below provide added display and storage space in the entrance hall.

Upper level:
1,795 square feet
Lower level:
866 square feet

ffectively dividing public and private spaces, this floor plan features a large living room with a sloped ceiling and an adjacent dining room. Both are attractive areas for entertaining guests. The bedrooms, including a master suite, are at the opposite end of the house. The homeowners will enjoy the terrace adjacent to the breakfast room, where meals can be served in warmer months. The downstairs is also reserved for family use. The raised-hearth fireplace in the family room has a window seat to match the one in the living room above. The space across from the family room could function as a home office, and the adjacent bathroom also qualifies it as a good guest room. Outside, twin gables dominate the Tudor-style facade.

A window seat to the right of the living-room fireplace is sure to be a popular spot for reading.

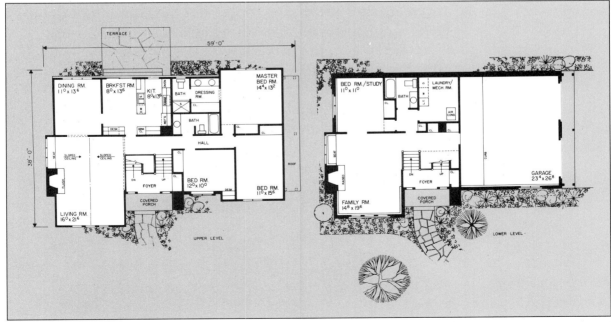

Main level:

1,143 square feet

Lower level:

770 square feet

Upper level:

792 square feet

everal updates of the typical floor plan can be seen here, notably replacement of the living room with a gathering room and addition of an activities room. Across the rear of the entire house runs a series of terraces that serves as outdoor living spaces during warm months. Four rooms have access to these terraces: the activities room, the gathering room, the dining room, and the family room. The kitchen, adjacent to an eating area, features a snack bar certain to simplify serving meals. Downstairs is a study that can also double as a guest bedroom with its conveniently located bathroom nearby. Three more bedrooms are provided on the upper level, including a master suite with a dressing room. Tudor-style detailing on the facade includes decorative half-timbering and a large chimney in the center.

The brick facade of the gathering room's fireplace extends to the sloped ceiling. French doors lead to the terrace.

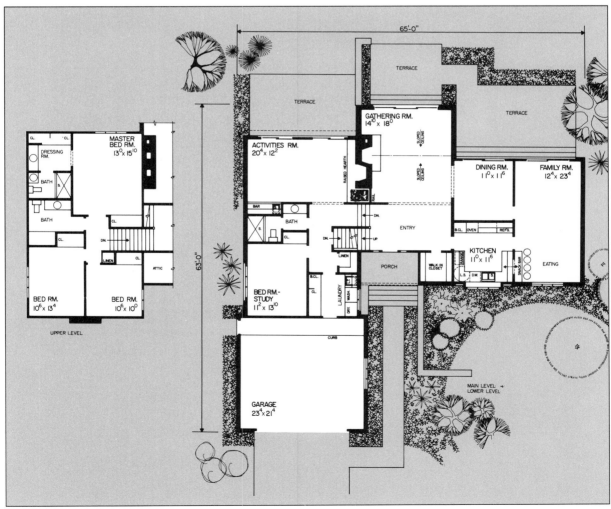

Single level:
2,747 square feet

udor-style detailing, as in diamond-shaped windowpanes and decorative half-timbering, merges here with contemporary ranch style. The resulting plan is both spacious and convenient. From the service entrance at the garage, there is immediate access to the kitchen. The home-owners can enjoy rear terrace areas from three separate locations—the kitchen nook, the family room, and the master suite. In this plan the living room and dining room are combined into one space featuring a fireplace and built-in shelving. Away from the major traffic patterns of the house is a study-office, which can double as a guest bedroom. Three additional bedrooms and a master suite, all equally convenient to a nearby bath, are included in this floor plan.

A corner fireplace in the family room features a raised brick hearth. The entry hall is beyond the doorway.

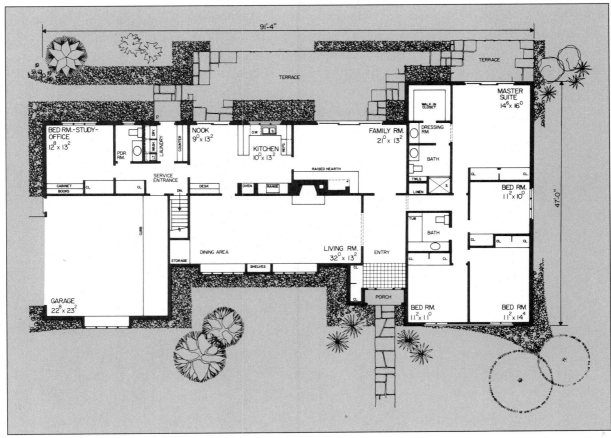

91'-4"

47'-0"

TERRACE

TERRACE

MASTER
SUITE
14⁶ x 16⁰

WALK-IN
CLOSET

BED RM.-STUDY-
OFFICE
12⁸ x 13²

NOOK
9⁰ x 13²

FAMILY RM.
21⁰ x 13²

DRESSING
RM.

PDR.
RM.

WASH DRY

LAUNDRY

COUNTER

KITCHEN
10⁰ x 13²

D.W.   S

REFG.

BATH

TWLS

CL.   CL.

CABINET

CL.   CL.

SERVICE
ENTRANCE

DESK

DN.

OVEN RANGE

RAISED HEARTH

LINEN

S

BED RM.
11² x 10⁰

BOOKS

CL.RB.

TUB

BATH

DINING AREA

LIVING RM.
32⁰ x 13²

ENTRY

CL.   CL.

STORAGE

SHELVES

GARAGE
22⁸ x 23²

PORCH

CL.

BED RM.
11² x 11⁰

BED RM.
11² x 14⁴

First floor:
1,922 square feet
Second floor:
890 square feet

Small terraces and covered porches make inviting niches in this plan. In addition to the porch at the front entryway, there is another off the breakfast room, accessible through sliding glass doors. The terraces off the master bedroom and living room extend the living space of those two areas. When the homeowners entertain, the living-room terrace can easily accommodate any overflow of guests. The smaller terrace off the master bedroom is ideal for reading or relaxing. The location of this room downstairs provides increased privacy. The kitchen layout promotes easy food preparation, and the pass-through between the kitchen and breakfast room makes serving informal meals convenient. The plan provides for three upstairs bedrooms, each with separate storage areas, including two walk-in closets.

A massive brick fireplace in the family room is complemented by imposing beams in the vaulted ceiling.

Main level:
889 square feet
Upper level:
960 square feet
Lower level:
936 square feet

 Both the street and the garden views of this house are equally pleasing, with Tudor-style detailing, such as diamond-shaped windowpanes that contribute to the facade's continuity. Decorative chimney pots and half-timbering are also welcome traditional touches. From the street there is little indication of the three levels of living space within. The main level is ideal for formal entertaining, with the living room located just through the entrance hall. From both this room and the dining room, guests enjoy direct access to the rear terrace. A short flight of stairs from the entrance hall leads to the upper-level sleeping area, which includes three bedrooms and a master suite with its own private balcony. Most communal activity will be on the lower level, where the large family room is located.

The living room fireplace acts as a centerpiece for a furniture grouping. Paneled walls add to this area's feeling of warmth.

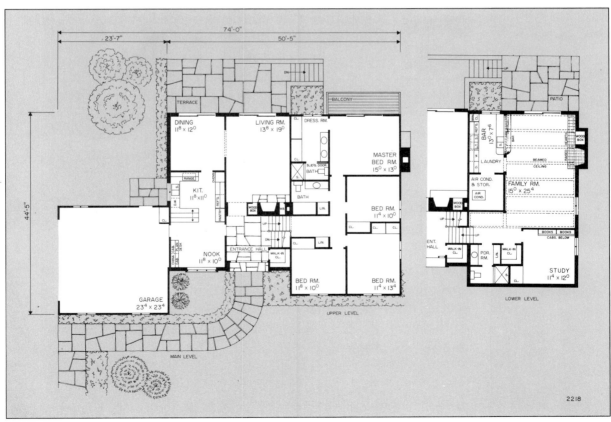

Main level:

1,801 square feet

Lower level:

1,061 square feet

This Tudor-style facade is unified by the repetition of certain design elements. The look of the casementlike windows, for instance, is repeated in the transom above the front door. Other traditional elements identified with this style include decorative half-timbering, a massive chimney, and partial stone cladding. Inside, the floor plan is well suited to the needs of homeowners with busy life-styles. For formal occasions guests can make use of the living room, with its sloped ceiling, fireplace, and built-in bookshelves. The dining room's sliding glass doors provide access to a balcony perfect for entertaining on warm summer nights. The master suite has its own balcony, as well as a dressing room and spacious closets. Downstairs, homeowners will enjoy the family room, with its raised-hearth fireplace and built-in cabinetry. The rear terrace is ideal for barbecues and informal parties.

A full wall of pantry space in the kitchen still allows room for a built-in desk. A work island aids in food preparation.

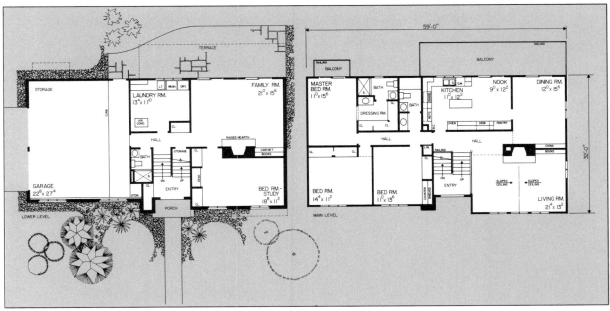

Single level:
2,790 square feet

ith the floor plan of a contemporary ranch home and details characteristic of the Tudor style, this home offers the best of both worlds. A large, multipaned window in the living room dominates the facade, mixing comfortably with other windows that feature diamond-shaped panes. A trio of terraces provides inviting settings for entertaining or simply reading and relaxing. The gathering room in the rear is aptly named, for it is where the family is sure to congregate. This space includes an eating area and a built-in desk. The adjoining terrace is accessible through sliding glass doors. Meals, whether formal or informal, will be easy to prepare in this kitchen, with its convenient work island. The dining room, separated from the living room by a through-fireplace, is only steps away. This plan provides for three bedrooms, one being a master suite with a spacious dressing room and double vanities.

The dining room shares a through-wall fireplace with the living room; the brick facade is an impressive and typically Tudor touch.

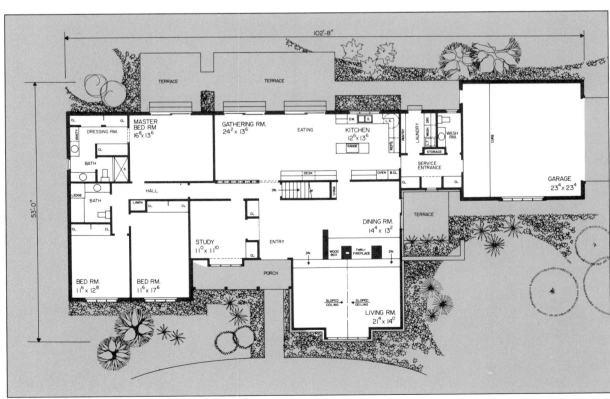

First floor:
1,718 square feet
Second floor:
1,147 square feet

In this plan the garage and kitchen are conveniently close so that unloading groceries doesn't involve a long trek. And placing the laundry room directly across from the kitchen confines work activities within one area of the house. Overnight guests will find the downstairs bedroom ideal not only because of the adjacent rear terrace and bathroom but also because of the privacy it provides. The cook has easy access to both the eating nook and the dining room. Upstairs, the sense of space in the already generous master suite is enhanced by the attached sitting room. Adjacent to the suite are a large walk-in closet, a vanity, and double sinks.

Located adjacent to the master suite is a sitting room with a view of the rear garden.

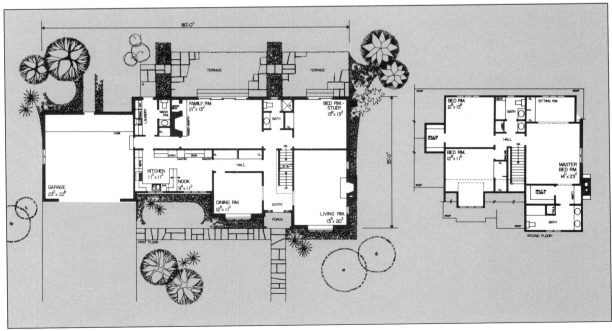

Single level:

2,919 square feet

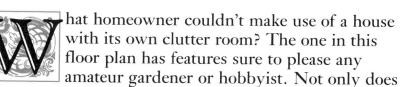

What homeowner couldn't make use of a house with its own clutter room? The one in this floor plan has features sure to please any amateur gardener or hobbyist. Not only does the room have its own potting area, but there is also a central island for other projects, a space for sewing, and even a washer and dryer. This plan's most prominent feature is nevertheless the greenhouse—accessible from both the clutter room and the country kitchen—which adds another 130 square feet to the plan's overall footage. Greenery and a few pieces of wicker will transform this space into the perfect retreat. The kitchen includes a snack bar ideal either for snacks or more informal meals. In the combination media room/ study there is an entire wall available for storage of electronic equipment. The living room, with its raised hearth and sloped ceiling, provides access to the rear terrace, as does the dining room. Features of the master suite include a walk-in closet, a built-in vanity, and a whirlpool tub.

A potting area in the clutter room of this plan is located conveniently adjacent to the greenhouse.

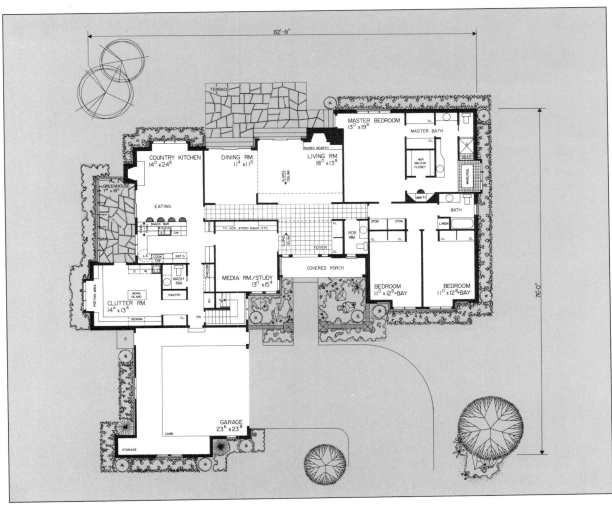

First floor:

1,490 square feet

Second floor:

1,474 square feet

 This traditional layout has a thoroughly modern floor plan, complete with a two-car garage and a library. To ensure privacy and quiet, the library is located away from the traffic patterns created by a busy family. The adjacent powder room is useful not only for someone in the library but for guests as well, since it is also near the entry. Upstairs, it's obvious that this plan was created to meet the needs of a large family. There is a total of six bedrooms, including a master suite with a dressing room, and there are plenty of built-in closets. The floor's centrally located other bathroom is easily accessible. On the ground floor, there's a family room featuring a fireplace with hearth and built-in woodbox. Across the rear of the house is a large terrace accessible from both the breakfast room and the living room by sliding glass doors. With such a floor plan, designed to accommodate a large family, there's little doubt that the mudroom, which doubles as a laundry room, will see plenty of use.

In the living room, an imposing fireplace features an elegant mantel. Windows flanking the fireplace add symmetry.

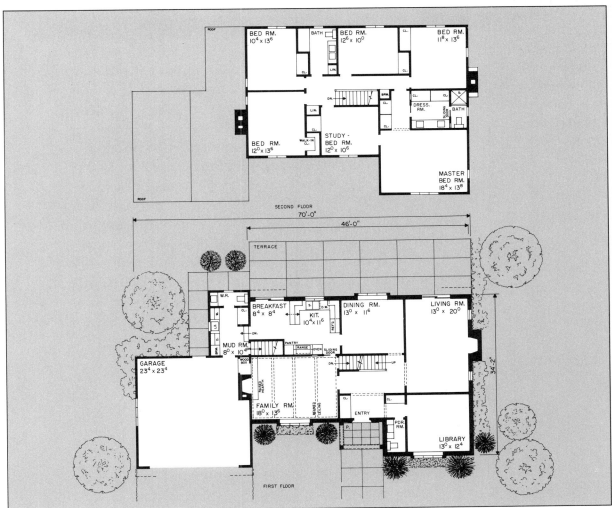

First floor:
1,617 square feet
Second floor:
1,348 square feet

The traditional Tudor detailing of the facade of this home disguises a floor plan that is altogether contemporary and certain to meet the needs of today's active family. The kitchen, which includes an eating area, also offers a practical work triangle. The spacious family room has access to the rear terrace, as does the dining room. Locating one of the house's four bedrooms on the first floor is a perfect arrangement for overnight guests, who will have the added convenience of their own private bath. This room might also double as a study or office. A second-floor lounge almost equal in size to the family room offers a quiet retreat for reading or relaxing. The master bedroom has built-in bookshelves and a separate dressing room. Access to a large attic storage area is provided from this level.

Beamed ceilings
and elaborate door
hardware add to the
rustic warmth and
intimacy of the
family room.

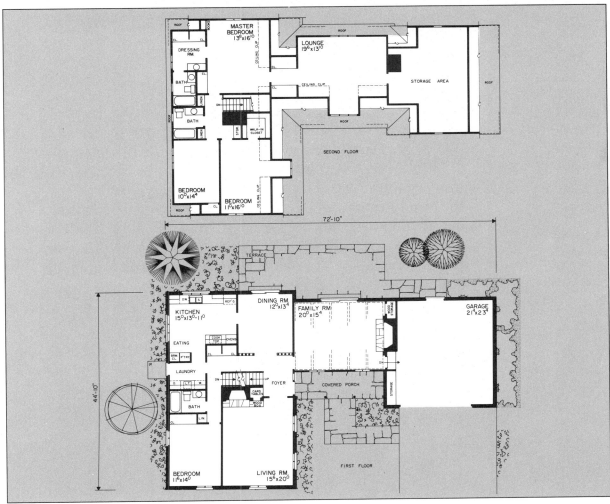

First floor:
1,512 square feet
Second floor:
1,480 square feet

 onvenience is a hallmark of this design, with its public and private spaces neatly separated. Guests can walk directly into the living room and then into the dining room for formal meals. Household activities will most likely center in the family room, which features a fireplace with a raised hearth. Flowing into this space is an eating nook. Both rooms have access to the terrace through sliding glass doors. The kitchen-nook includes a pantry and a built-in desk. For added privacy there is a study, located away from the busy kitchen. Upstairs, this plan offers four bedrooms, one being a large master suite with a spacious walk-in closet. On the same floor, there is a sitting room for quiet moments.

A view into the family room from the sunny kitchen nook. The bifold doors may be closed for added privacy.

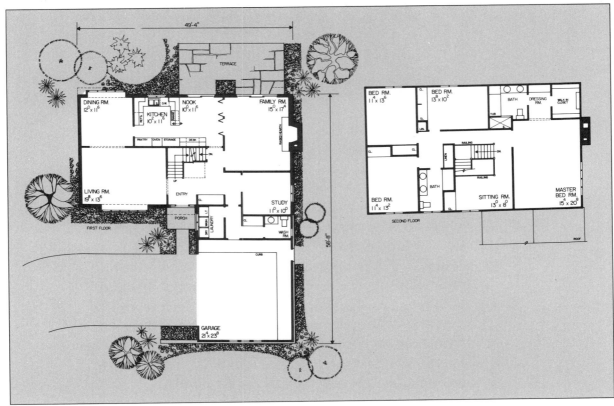

Lower level:
1,168 square feet
Upper level:
1,882 square feet

 he strong Tudor detailing on the facade of this house—decorative half-timbering and cross-gables—gives little hint of the contemporary conveniences inside. Such amenities extend to the rear of the structure, where a large deck and covered terrace below it provide outdoor living space. Homeowners will find entertaining in this house a delight. After a formal meal in the dining room, guests can stroll out on the deck and relax. Family members can also enjoy access to the deck from the breakfast room. Below, the covered terrace is appealing because of its contiguity to the family room. This plan also offers a special feature guaranteed to please the do-it-yourselfer: a workshop on the lower level.

A pass-through between kitchen and breakfast room makes serving meals easier and more convenient.

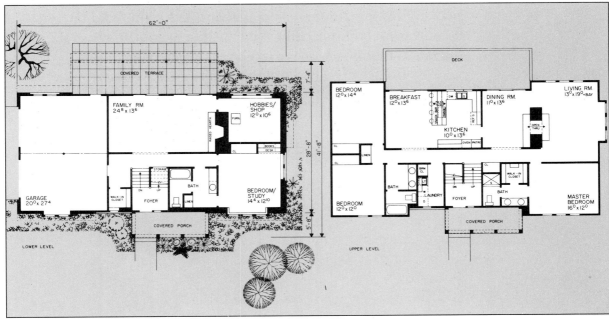

LOWER LEVEL

UPPER LEVEL

First floor:

1,646 square feet

Second floor:

1,487 square feet

he formal look of this home, with its traditional stone and brick facade, is matched inside with airy, contemporary spaces certain to please today's active family. Two fireplaces, in the living room and the family room, add to the general feeling of comfort in the house. The kitchen provides an ideal work triangle, and adjacent to it is a sun-filled breakfast room complemented by skylights. Serving informal meals is made simple by the kitchen layout: One counter can easily double as a buffet. Guests will enjoy the convenience of a powder room just off the foyer. The large two-car garage includes storage areas. Upstairs, double vanity sinks and a spacious walk-in closet are prominent features of the master suite. Three other bedrooms and another bath are included in this plan.

Skylights and a slanted ceiling add drama to the breakfast room, with its multipaned windows, seen here from the kitchen.

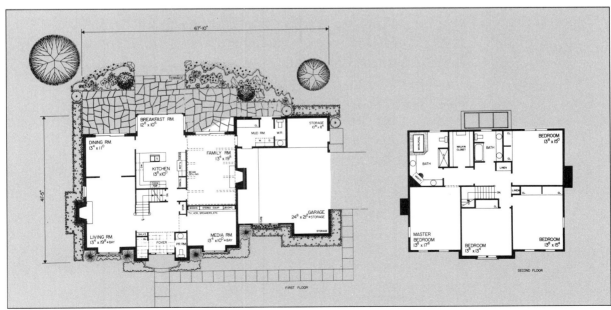

Main level:
1,274 square feet

Upper level:
960 square feet

Lower level:
936 square feet

 variety of outdoor living spaces complements the traditional design of this house. In warmer months the family room and adjacent terrace on the main level can merge to accommodate a flow of guests. On the upper level, a private balcony off the master bedroom is perfect for early-morning coffee, reading the newspaper, or just relaxing. Another terrace has been placed on the lower level, accessible from both the laundry/sewing room and bedroom/study, which features a built-in desk and bookcases. On this same level, a separate game room is sure to become a gathering place for family and friends. To avoid having to make trips to the upstairs kitchen, the planners have placed a snack bar and a pair of refrigerators in this area. The facade of the house still conveys an overall look of Tudor style, with its decorative half-timbering, diamond-shaped windowpanes, and gable detailing.

A fireplace with curved brick detailing is the focal point of the living room. This space is separated from the dining area by a raised balustrade.

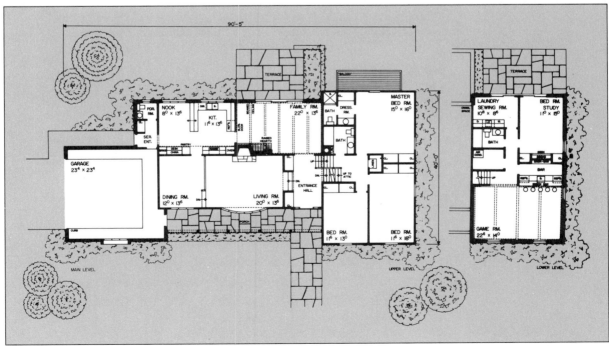

Main level:
1,220 square feet
Upper level:
1,344 square feet
Lower level:
659 square feet

 Light-filled interiors and a feeling of openness are noticeable throughout this design, from its multitude of windows and sliding glass doors. There is a solarium, perfect for relaxing or eating informal meals, located off the dining room. Sliding glass doors give access from the master bedroom to its balcony. For the cook, serious or otherwise, there is a dream kitchen. At its center is a spacious work island conveniently located within the conventional work triangle. The kitchen area extends to include a breakfast room accessible to the rear terrace. A built-in buffet, china cabinet, and pantry are also featured. The basement, convenient now for storage, could convert into a workroom.

Elements of Tudor style, notably the diamond-shaped windowpanes, receive a contemporary interpretation in the solarium.

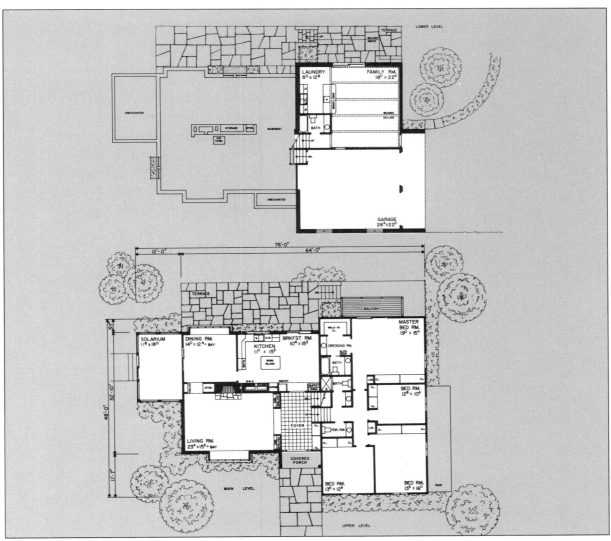

First floor:
1,656 square feet
Second floor:
1,565 square feet

The best way to describe this design, with its abundance of Tudor detailing, is to call it stately. The exterior cladding is a mixture of stone on the first floor and decorative half-timbering on the second, a combination often enough found in this style of architecture. Inside is the best of contemporary convenience. An unusually large equipment-storage area to the rear of the garage is spacious enough for the needs of any homeowner-gardener. The mudroom off the garage has a washroom and built-ins for added convenience. The first floor features two fireplaces: one in the living room, the other (with a raised hearth) in the family room. The living room and dining room both overlook a rear terrace accessible through sliding glass doors. On the second floor are six bedrooms, including the master suite. Ample closet space and three separate linen closets are provided.

Built-in book-shelves in the library help ease storage problems, as do the raised-panel cabinets below.

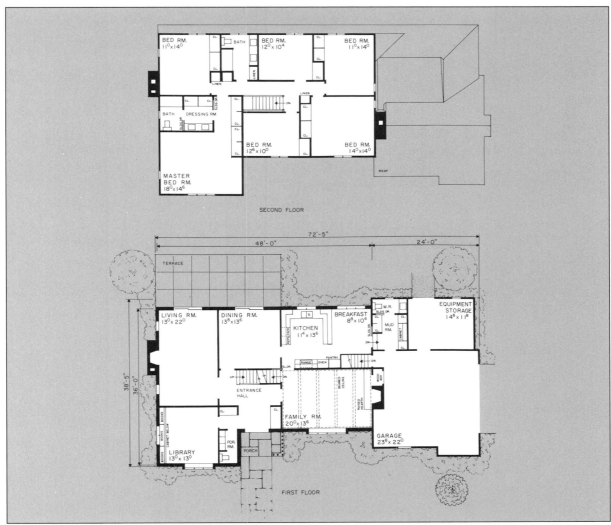

SECOND FLOOR

FIRST FLOOR

First floor:
1,797 square feet
Second floor:
1,514 square feet

he imposing facade of this house is accented by a variety of Tudor-style details: decorative half-timbering (some of it curved), chimney pots, stone wall cladding, and gable ornaments. Guests can enter from the large foyer into the living room, dining room, or family room. A large terrace extending across the rear is accessible through sliding glass doors in the living room and dining room. Homeowners will appreciate the large family room complete with beamed ceilings, a raised hearth, and a built-in woodbox. The first floor also features a combination office-den, placed away from traffic patterns, and a more formal library for reading and relaxing. Six bedrooms, including a master suite with its own dressing room, are located on the second floor. Part of the family's storage needs are solved by the large attic space accessible by disappearing stairs in the garage.

A view from the staircase in the foyer toward the entrance. The diamond-shaped panes in the front door window are reminiscent of Tudor style.

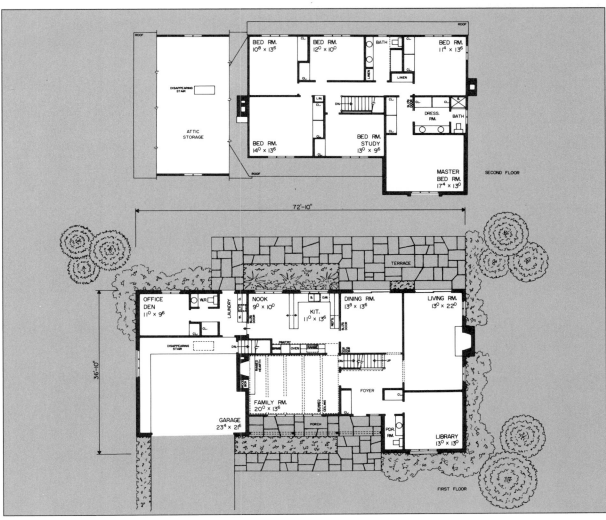

DISAPPEARING STAIR

ATTIC STORAGE

BED RM.
10⁸ x 13⁶

BED RM.
12⁰ x 10⁰

BATH

BED RM.
11⁴ x 13⁶

LINEN

LINEN

BED RM.
14⁰ x 13⁶

BED RM.
STUDY
13⁰ x 9⁶

DRESS. RM.

BATH

MASTER BED RM.
17⁴ x 13⁰

SECOND FLOOR

72'-10"

36'-10"

TERRACE

OFFICE DEN
11⁰ x 9⁶

WR

LAUNDRY

NOOK
9⁰ x 10⁰

KIT.
11⁰ x 13⁶

DINING RM.
13⁸ x 13⁶

LIVING RM.
13⁰ x 22⁰

DISAPPEARING STAIR

OVEN

FOYER

CL.

FAMILY RM.
20⁰ x 13⁶

GARAGE
23⁴ x 2⁶

PORCH

PDR. RM.

LIBRARY
13⁰ x 13⁰

FIRST FLOOR

First floor:
1,985 square feet
Second floor:
1,659 square feet

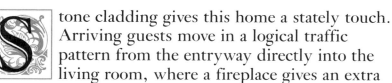

Stone cladding gives this home a stately touch. Arriving guests move in a logical traffic pattern from the entryway directly into the living room, where a fireplace gives an extra touch of comfort. Through the living room is the family room, and next to it the dining room. Both spaces offer a view of the rear terrace. For added convenience there is a powder room near the entry hall. Homeowners will delight in this floor plan, which provides a service entrance adjoining the laundry room, with its own counter for folding clothes. In the kitchen an island has been incorporated into the traditional work triangle to make food preparation easier. Upstairs, double vanities and lots of closet space are featured in the master suite.

A bay window in the second floor's master bedroom is an ideal spot for reading, relaxing or, in this adaptation, playing the piano.

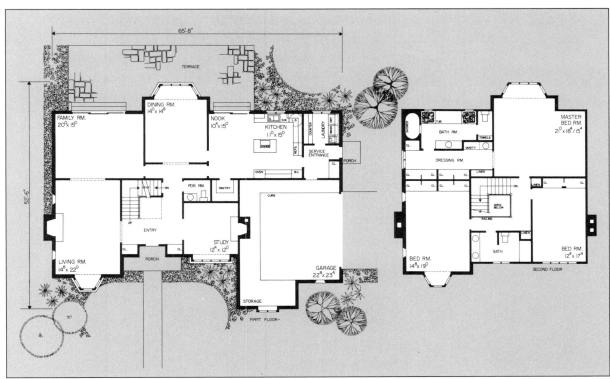

First floor:
1,680 square feet
Second floor:
1,165 square feet
Apartment level:
867 square feet

or homeowners who may share space with an older family member, this is an ideal floor plan. The arrangement provides for an almost separate apartment complete with a living room, bedroom, small kitchen, bath, and even a small balcony. In the main house are four bedrooms, including a master suite with a dressing room and a pair of walk-in closets. Downstairs, in the kitchen, the cook can continue preparing meals while enjoying conversation with family and friends in the adjoining family room. French doors dominate two walls of the family room and provide a view of the rear terrace. The study has thoughtfully been placed away from areas with heavy traffic. The dining room has its own access to the terrace, making it ideal for entertaining guests.

Open to the family room, this kitchen features counter space that serves as a room divider.

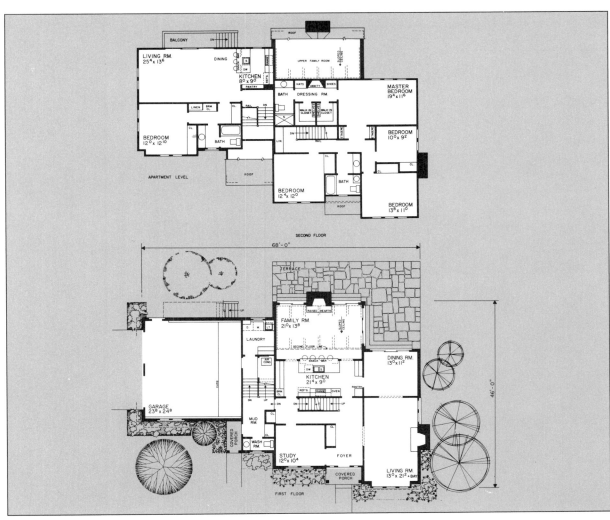

MANORS

Tracing its style to monarchs, Tudor has become synonymous with grand manor houses. Today's versions maintain their architectural integrity and offer the latest amenities.

Plan 2356, page 184

First floor:

1,372 square feet

Second floor:

1,245 square feet

Both the public and private areas of this house offer ideal plans for traffic flow. The homeowners will undoubtedly spend much of their time in the breakfast room, family room, porch, and nearby hobby/storage room. Guests can easily circulate between the more formal living room and the dining room. The kitchen, which conveniently separates the dining room from the breakfast room, features an ideal work triangle. The cook will also enjoy having a work island that can double as a buffet for informal meals. Upstairs, the master suite has its own whirlpool tub plus a dressing room with built-in closets and shelves for linens. The three other bedrooms, on this level, include one with a built-in desk and shelves, perfect for the student in the family. A second bathroom is located conveniently between two of the bedrooms.

The family room gets plenty of natural light; its centerpiece is a fireplace with a raised hearth.

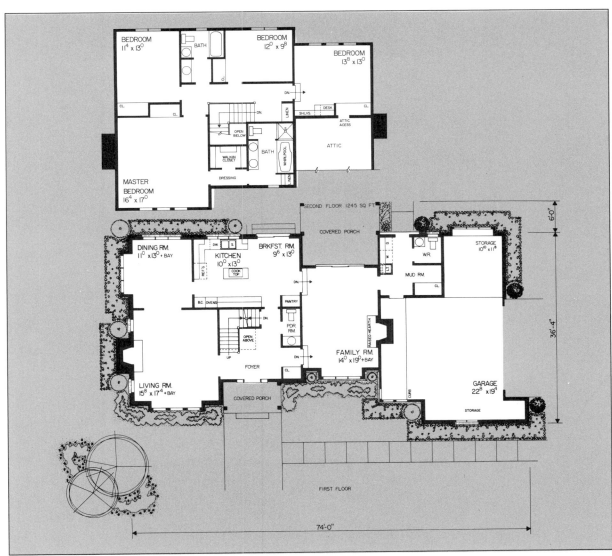

BEDROOM
11⁴ x 13⁰

BATH

BEDROOM
12⁰ x 9⁸

BEDROOM
13⁸ x 13⁰

CL.

CL.

DN.

DESK

SHLVS.

CL.

DN.

LINER

ATTIC
ACESS

OPEN
BELOW

WHIRLPOOL

ATTIC

WALK-IN
CLOSET

BATH

LINEN

MASTER
BEDROOM
16⁴ x 17⁰

DRESSING

SECOND FLOOR 1245 SQ FT

COVERED PORCH

6'-0"

DINING RM.
11⁰ x 13⁰ + BAY

DW

S

KITCHEN
10⁰ x 13⁰

BRKFST. RM.
9⁶ x 13⁰

STORAGE
10⁰ x 11⁸

REF'G

COOK
TOP

DN.

W.R.

MUD RM.

B.C. OVENS

PANTRY

DN.

CL.

OPEN
ABOVE

PDR.
RM.

36'-4"

UP

FAMILY RM.
14⁰ x 19⁰ + BAY

DN.

FOYER

CL.

LIVING RM.
15⁸ x 17⁴ + BAY

COVERED PORCH

CURB

GARAGE
22⁸ x 19⁴

STORAGE

FIRST FLOOR

74'-0"

First floor:
1,692 square feet
Second floor:
1,445 square feet

In this house the living room opens to the second floor, giving the space a grand scale. This feeling has already been accentuated on the facade, with its traditional Tudor details of a dominant chimney and decorative half-timbering. Both the dining room and the breakfast nook offer access to the rear terrace. The kitchen, which features a work island, has a number of built-ins, including a desk and china cabinets. This floor plan is ideal for entertaining, as guests can circulate easily from living room to dining room to terrace. The family room will also be a center of activity. Snacks can be served conveniently here because of a pass-through to the kitchen, and the adjacent terrace will prove attractive to both homeowners and guests. Three bedrooms, including a master suite, are provided in the plan for the second floor. There is also a study here, with its location well planned to be away from the house's major areas of traffic.

From the balcony railing on the second floor there is a view of the living room below.

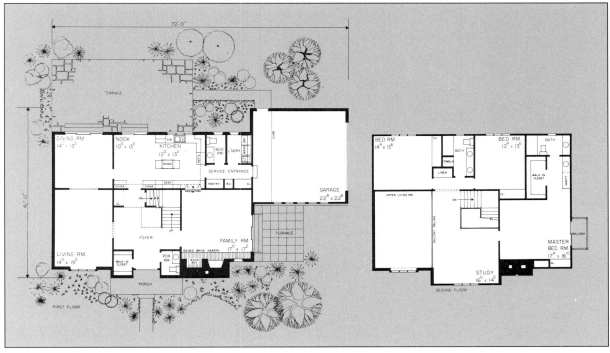

First floor:
1,650 square feet
Second floor:
1,507 square feet

arge, inviting rooms perfect for entertaining help to distinguish this floor plan. For the convenience of visitors there is both a powder room and a walk-in closet just off the entry hall. Guests can circulate easily from the living room to the nearby family room with its beamed ceiling, fireplace, and sliding glass doors that provide access to a covered porch and terrace. The divider between the breakfast room and the kitchen makes serving convenient. There is ample storage on both floors, with one space located off the garage and a second in the area above. The plan provides for five bedrooms on the second floor, with one that might double as a study. The spacious master suite features its own dressing room and plenty of closet space.

In an upstairs bed-room a window seat offers a cozy retreat for a nap or just curling up with a book.

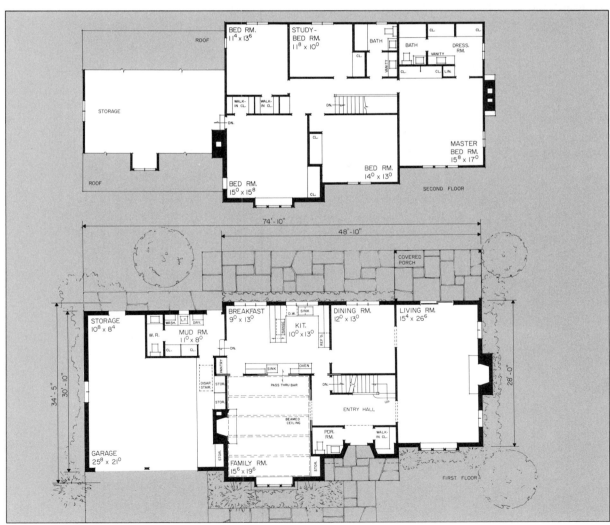

Single level:
3,161 square feet

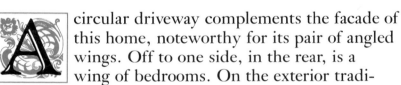

circular driveway complements the facade of this home, noteworthy for its pair of angled wings. Off to one side, in the rear, is a wing of bedrooms. On the exterior traditional Tudor details are in evidence, such as diamond-shaped window panes and large chimneys with decorative pots. In the rear of the house, a gently curving terrace is accessible from several rooms. The master bedroom features a private "quiet" terrace all its own. The plan provides for three fireplaces: one in the living room, another in the family room, and a third in the master suite. Built-in bookshelves with cabinets below them are set on either side of the living-room fireplace. A bathroom has been placed between two of the bedrooms for the added convenience of the occupants of each room.

A fireplace in the master bedroom establishes a focal point for the room and provides a comfortable spot for relaxing.

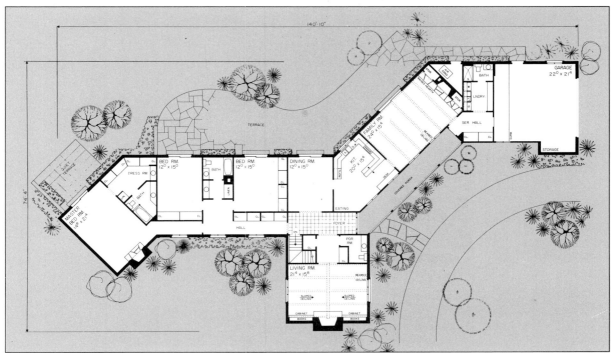

First floor:
2,496 square feet
Second floor:
958 square feet

The imposing facade of this home is dominated by a flat-roofed castellated tower in the shape of an octagon. This architectural form, which can be traced to the Middle Ages, blends with traditional Tudor details such as decorative half-timbering and diamond-shaped window panes. The castellations are repeated on a brick wall at one end of a rear terrace, adding continuity to the facade. Inside, both the living room and the family room feature fireplaces. A terrace has been conveniently located to serve both rooms. At the opposite side of the house, another terrace is accessible from no fewer than three bedrooms, including the master suite. Upstairs, a balcony is shared by two additional bedrooms. A combination study/lounge features built-in bookshelves and cabinets.

T he circle-head front door in the foyer is complemented by the shape of a nearby niche, which is an ideal spot for displaying flowers and ceramics.

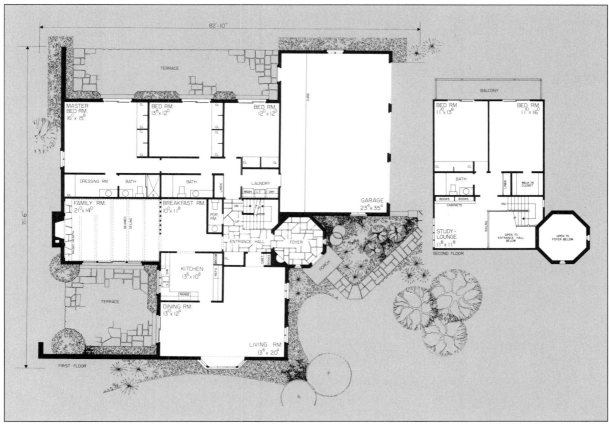

179

First floor:
2,855 square feet
Second floor:
955 square feet

he ultimate in homeowner privacy is provided by this floor plan, with its second-story space allocated exclusively to a master suite. Because of the placement of two sets of dormers, light can filter into opposite sides of the room. This space also features separate bathrooms and dressing rooms as well as a number of built-ins, such as bookcases in the four dormers, and a pair of chests. Downstairs, the family room and kitchen are adjacent, with a snack bar to divide the two spaces and make meal serving easy. A trio of terraces off various locations downstairs virtually extends the living space to the outdoors. There is one terrace off the family room, another off the kitchen nook, and a third accessible from the living room. A library with built-in bookshelves might also serve as a bedroom for weekend guests.

Exposed beams in the ceiling of the master bedroom add drama to a space already distinguished by having its own private staircase.

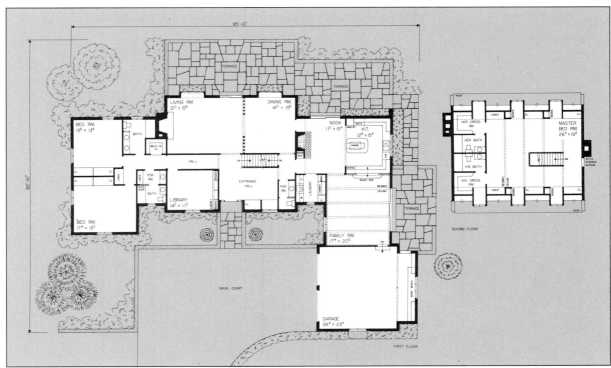

First floor:
2,044 square feet
Second floor:
1,962 square feet

 variety of ornamented gables distinguishes this postmodern/Victorian facade noteworthy for its large chimney. Inside, a number of details in the floor plan help make life convenient for the homeowner. The kitchen features not only an island but also a built-in desk. A bar and sink in the family room, which is perfect for light snacks, is certain to become a gathering spot for guests. The library features an entire wall of bookshelves. In the walk-in closet off the receiving hall there is even a special location to store card tables. Upstairs, the master suite includes separate baths, with a shower in His and a tub in Hers. Closet space hasn't been overlooked, including shoe storage. Throughout the house, both upstairs and down, a series of covered porches and balconies helps to extend the living space.

The height of the
family room allows
the fireplace, with
the floor-to-ceiling
windows on either
side, to dominate
the space.

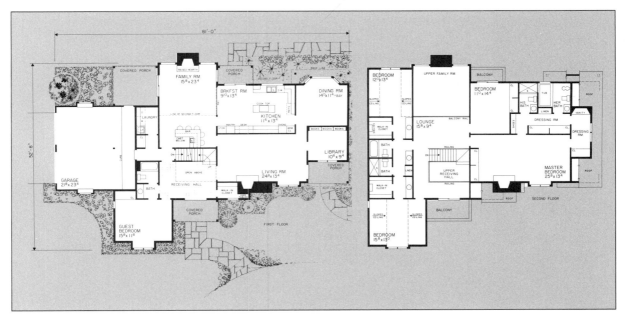

First Floor:
1,969 square feet
Second floor:
1,702 square feet

ruly a manor in both scale and architectural detail, this house also offers extraordinary convenience for today's family. Indeed, the home's centerpiece is a two-story family room, also visible from a landing on the second floor. From a nook adjacent to the family room, sliding glass doors lead out to the rear terrace. On the other side of this room, two more doors open to a comfortable, covered porch. The library-study, off the living room, features built-in cabinets and bookcases. A first-floor guest bedroom has its own bath to ensure privacy. The house's four other bedrooms, including a master suite with its own dressing room, are on the second floor, which also features a lounge for reading or relaxing, and an extra storage closet. Guests will appreciate the receiving hall's proportions, which emphasize the manorlike feel of this space.

Stretching from the manteltop to the ceiling, tall windows with diamond-shaped panes enhance the family room's stately proportions. Beamed ceilings and a raised hearth contribute to this area's impressive feel.

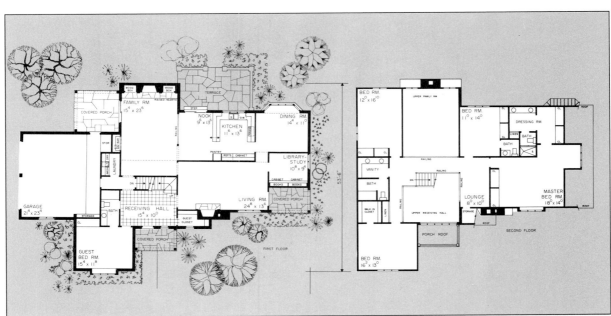

185

First floor:
2,557 square feet

Second floor:
1,939 square feet

 This multi-gabled facade with its traditional Tudor details gives little hint of the contemporary convenience featured inside. The latest in open-plan kitchen design is provided, with an island that allows the cook to converse with family and friends. The island might also serve as a buffet for meals served in the adjoining breakfast room. There are built-ins throughout the house, such as a cabinet in the living room and china storage in the dining room. Nearby there is a feature not often seen in today's floor plans: a butler's pantry for storage of serving pieces and flatware. And what homeowner wouldn't relish the addition of the second story's most prominent feature, a whirlpool tub in the bath of the master suite? Three other bedrooms upstairs include a guest bedroom with its own dressing room and bath.

A dramatic circular staircase greets visitors to this house; the entrance to the gathering room is beneath the staircase. On the second floor, double doors open to the master suite.

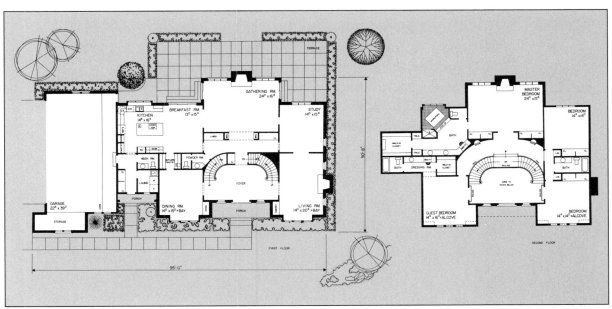

First floor:
2,991 square feet
Second floor:
1,802 square feet

Victorian details dominate the exterior of this house. Inside, the floor plan provides for a series of views that accentuate the large, comfortable rooms. From the foyer a visitor can look directly into the great room, with its handsome fireplace. The sitting room of the master suite lets the homeowners enjoy a view of the house's porch and garden beyond. The same is true of the morning room, with its four walls of windows. Located conveniently near the morning room is the kitchen, with its work island and adjacent butler's pantry. Across from the formal dining room is the library. The downstairs master suite, planned for added privacy and convenience, has its own whirlpool tub as well as a pair of large walk-in closets. Upstairs, one of the bedrooms functions as a sort of mini-master suite, with not only a private bath and walk-in closet but an alcove for a computer. Two of the three other bedrooms also feature private baths. The lounge, complete with fireplace and built-in bookshelves, makes an ideal place for relaxing.

A graceful staircase enhances the foyer of this home, illuminated by a fanlight set above the double entry doors.

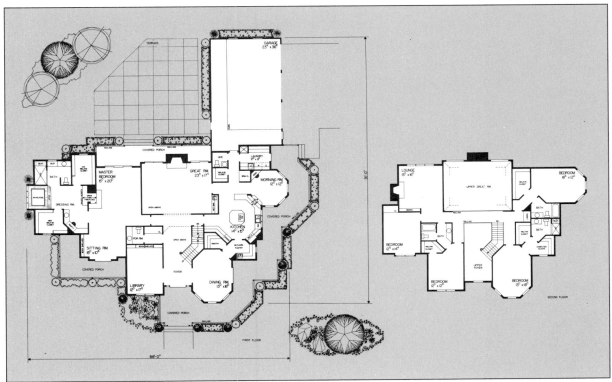

First floor:
3,679 square feet
Second floor:
1,461 square feet

With a master suite as luxurious as the one offered in this floor plan, homeowners may find it difficult to leave the space. Not only does the area feature its own fireplace (one of three in the house), but it also has sliding glass doors that lead to a rear deck, an ideal location for a breakfast table and chairs. This suite has His and Hers dressing rooms and enormous walk-in closets. Located conveniently nearby is the media room, with its own built-in bar. Both the formal dining room and the informal breakfast nook are easily accessible from the kitchen. Added features of this area include a work island, a built-in desk, and a butler's pantry. A series of skylights is set above a portion of the rear deck. This space is accessible from the family room and breakfast nook through sliding glass doors. Three bedrooms and a lounge are included in the second-level plan, along with a large attic for storage.

A trio of doors in the living room features fanlights above them. From these doors the homeowners and their guests can step out onto a rear deck.

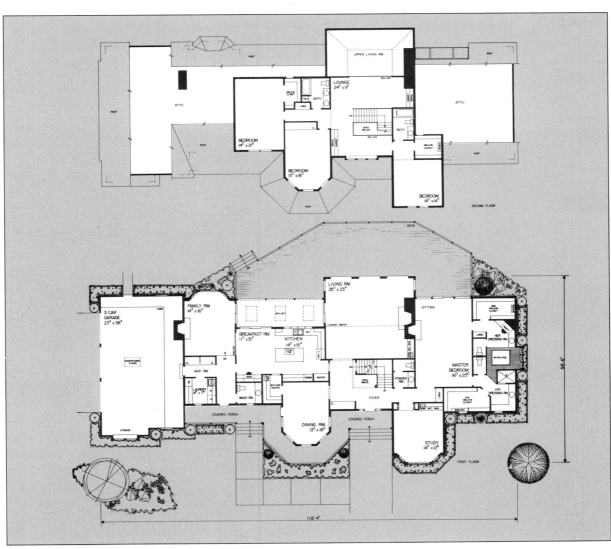

First floor:
3,736 square feet
Second floor:
2,264 square feet

 series of half-round windows dominates the facade of this stylish brick residence. The double-door entry is dominated by an elliptical fanlight with sidelights. Inside there is a luxury of space, with a morning room, gathering room, formal dining room, and a clutter room, all designed around a large kitchen complete with work island, built-in desk, and nearby pantry. Special features include sloped glass above the eating area in the morning room, plus a built-in bar, sculpture platform, and pair of niches in the gathering room. For added privacy, the master suite in this plan is located in its own wing on the first level. This space is indeed the perfect retreat. It features its own spa-exercise area and whirlpool tub, with a courtyard and a covered porch for relaxing. Four bedrooms are featured on the second level, along with an activity room that has a built-in soda fountain and piano niche.

The formal dining area provides a view of the foyer, with its imposing front doorway.

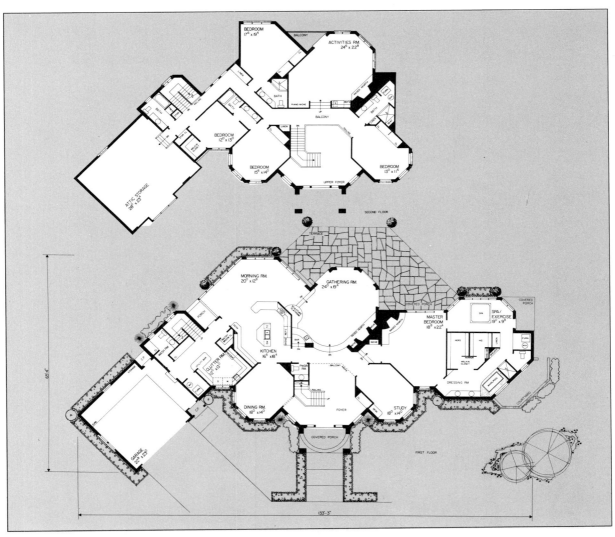

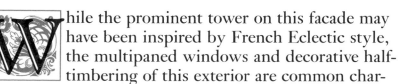

First floor:
4,195 square feet

Second floor:
2,094 square feet

While the prominent tower on this facade may have been inspired by French Eclectic style, the multipaned windows and decorative half-timbering of this exterior are common characteristics of Tudor architecture. This design offers a distinctive entry courtyard that has a pocket garden ideal for growing small cutting plants or herbs. Once inside the foyer, drama awaits in the form of a multi-sided gathering room that overlooks the rear garden and is open to the second floor. The first floor includes a media room with an entire wall for electronic equipment, as well as a morning room, which makes an ideal place for lingering over a cup of coffee or the newspaper. In the kitchen there is a work island that could also double as an informal buffet. His and Hers baths are special features of the downstairs master suite. Three bedrooms, a study, and a sitting room are provided in the second-floor plan.

A small sitting room off the master suite features a series of windows dramatically angled to take in the views.

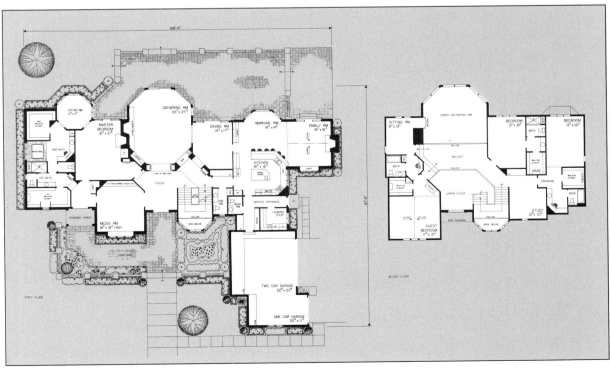

First floor:

4,274 square feet

Second floor:

3,008 square feet

 Baronial is the only way to describe this imposing home with its variety of Tudor details, including cross-gables, decorative half-timbering, and enormous chimneys. Once inside, visitors may first notice the circular staircase that dominates the foyer. The first level includes such distinctive spaces as a conversation room, a media center, a music alcove, and a telephone center. A total of three fireplaces ensures the comfort of both homeowners and guests. Two areas of garage space provide parking enough for three vehicles. The kitchen has its own work island, a pantry and separate walk-in butler's pantry, and even a barbecue grill. On the second level are other spaces not found in a typical floor plan, such as a combination nursery/exercise/storage area. The four other bedrooms on this floor offer a special luxury: Each has its own private bathroom.

From the dining room there is a view of the dramatic entryway, with multipaned expanses of glass on two levels.

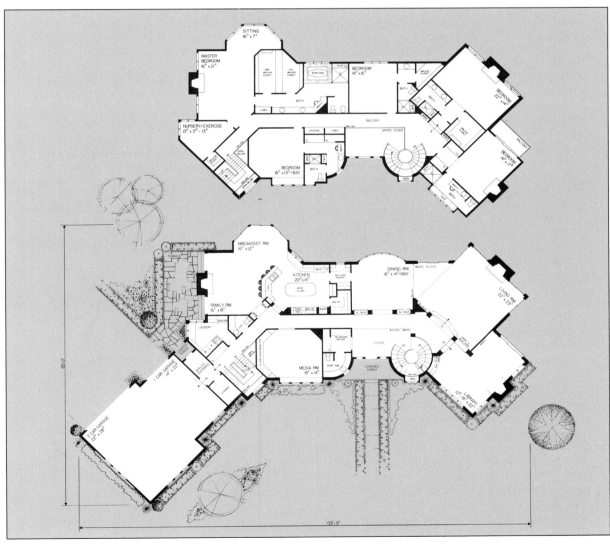

electing the most suitable house plan for your family is a matter of matching your needs, tastes, and life-style with one of the many designs offered here. When you study the floor plans and blueprints that you may order, remember that they are simply two-dimensional representations of what will eventually become a three-dimensional reality.

Basic floor plans are easy to read. Rooms are clearly labeled, with their dimensions given in feet and inches. Most symbols are logical and self-explanatory: The location of bathroom fixtures, planters, fireplaces, tile floors, cabinets and counters, sinks, appliances, closets, and sloped or beamed ceilings will be obvious.

A blueprint, though more detailed than a floor plan, is also easy to read; all it demands is concentration. The blueprints offered here come on many large sheets, each containing a different kind of information. One sheet contains foundation and excavation drawings, another a precise plot plan. Elevations sheets deal with the exterior walls of the house; section drawings show precise dimensions, fittings, doors, windows, and roof structures.

Detailed floor plans give the construction information needed by your contractor. Separate from the blueprints, but an important part of the package, is a lengthy materials list, with sizes and quantities for all necessary components. Using this list, the contractor and his suppliers can help calculate costs for you.

When you first study a floor plan or blueprint, imagine that you are walking through the house. By visualizing each room in three dimensions, you can transform the technical data and symbols into something like the real room.

Start at the front door. It's preferable to have a foyer or entrance hall in which to receive guests. A closet is desirable; a powder room is another plus.

Look for good traffic circulation. You should not have to pass all the way through one main room to reach another. From the entrance area you should have direct access to the three principal areas of a house—the living, working, and sleeping zones. For example, a foyer might provide separate entrances to the living room, kitchen, patio, and a hallway or staircase leading to the bedrooms.

Study the layout of each zone. Most people expect the living room to be protected from cross traffic. On the other hand, the kitchen should connect with the dining room and perhaps also the utility room, basement, garage, patio or deck, and a secondary entrance. A homemaker whose work day is centered around the kitchen may have special requirements: a window that faces the backyard, a clear view of the family room where children play, a convenient garage or driveway entrance that allows for a short trip with groceries, or laundry facilities close at hand. Check for efficient placement of kitchen cabinets, counters, and appliances. Is there enough room in the kitchen to eat there, or does it have a dining nook? This part of the house may also contain a family room or a den—bedroom—office. It's usually an advantage to have a bathroom or powder room.

Study the sleeping quarters. Are the bedrooms situated where you want them? You may prefer the master bedroom near the children's room, or you may want it as far from there as possible. Is there at least one closet per person in each bedroom, or a double one for a couple? Bathrooms should be convenient to each bedroom—if not adjoining them, then with hallway access and on the same floor.

As you study the overall floor plan, you may encounter a staircase, indicated by a set of parallel lines, with the number of lines equaling the number of steps. An arrow labeled "up" means that the staircase leads to a higher level, and one pointing down shows that it leads to a lower level. Staircases in a split-level have up and down arrows on the same staircase, because the two main levels are depicted in one drawing and any extra levels in another.

Notice the location of the stairways. Is too much floor space lost to them? Will you find yourself making too many trips?

Once you are familiar with the relative positions of the rooms, look for such structural details as

- sufficient uninterrupted wall space for furniture arrangement
- adequate room dimensions
- potential heating or cooling problems—that is, a room over a garage or next to the laundry
- window and door placement designed for good ventilation and natural light
- location of doorways that avoids having a basement staircase or a bathroom in view of the dining room
- adequate auxiliary space such as closets, storage, bathrooms, and countertops
- separation of activity areas, so noise from the recreation room does not disturb sleeping children or a parent at work.

As you complete your mental walk through the house, bear in mind your family's long-range needs. A good house plan will allow for some adjustments now and additions in the future.

Each member of your family may find the listing of his or her favorite home features a most helpful exercise. Why not try it?

contractor is part craftsman, part businessman, and part magician. As the person who will transform your dreams and drawings into a finished house, he will be responsible for the budget and the quality of the workmanship, and for finding solutions to the problems that occur naturally in the course of construction. Choose carefully.

There are two types of residential contractors: the *construction company* and the *carpenter-builder*, often called a general contractor. Each of these types has advantages and disadvantages.

The carpenter-builder works directly on the job as the field foreman. Because his background is that of a craftsman, his workmanship will probably be good, but his paperwork may be slow or sloppy. His overhead—which you pay for—is less than that of a large construction company. However, if the job drags on beyond schedule for any reason, his interest may flag, because your project may be overlapping his next job and eroding his profits.

Construction companies handle several projects simultaneously. They have an office staff to keep the paperwork moving, and an army of subcontractors they know they can count on. Though you are normally assured that they will meet deadlines, they may sacrifice workmanship to do so. Because they emphasize efficiency, they may be less personal to work with than a general contractor. Many will not work with an individual unless he is represented by an architect.

To find a reliable contractor, start by asking friends who have built homes or additions to their homes. Check with local lumberyards and building-supply outlets for names of other candidates.

Once you have several names in hand, ask the chamber of commerce, Better Business Bureau, or local department of consumer affairs for information these groups might have.

Set up an interview with the potential candidates. Ask to see projects that both are completed as well as in progress, emphasizing that you are interested in projects comparable to yours.

Ask each contractor for bank references, from both his commercial bank and any other lender he has worked with. If he is in good financial standing, he should have no qualms about giving you this information. Ask if he offers a warranty on the structure (some offer as much as a ten-year warranty).

Ask for references, realizing that no contractor will give you the name of a dissatisfied customer. Although previous clients may be pleased with a contractor's work overall, they may well have specific complaints about workmanship or the contractor's work habits. Ask.

Talk to each of the candidates about fees. Most work on a "cost plus" basis; that is, the basic cost of the project—materials, subcontractor's services, wages of those working directly on the project, but not office help—plus his fee. Some have a fixed fee, while others work on a percentage of the basic cost. A fixed fee is usually better for you if you can get one. If a contractor works on a percentage basis, ask for a cost breakdown on the best estimate and keep very careful track as the work progresses. A crafty contractor can always use a cost overrun to his advantage when working on a percentage.

If the top two or three candidates are willing to submit competitive bids, give each a copy of the plans and your specifications for materials. If they are not each working from the same guidelines, the competitive bids will be of little value. Give each the same deadline for turning in a bid (two or three weeks is a reasonable period).

The method just described sounds fair and orderly, but it is not always the best approach, especially if you are inexperienced. You may want to review the bids with your architect, if you have one, or your lender, to discuss which to accept. They may not recommend the lowest bid; it does not necessarily mean that you will get quality with economy.

If the bids are relatively close, the most important consideration may not be money at all. How easily you can talk with a contractor and whether or not he inspires confidence are important considerations to take into account.

Once you have your financing, you can sign a contract with the builder. Most have their own contract forms, but it is advisable to have a lawyer draw one up and use that rather than the builder's or, at least, have the lawyer review the builder's contract.

A good contract should include the following:

- plans and sketches of the work to be done, subject to your approval
- a list of materials, including quantity, brand names, style or serial numbers (do not permit any "or equal" clauses that will allow the contractor to make substitutions)
- the terms—who (you, or the lender?) pays whom and when
- a production schedule
- the contractor's certification of insurance for workmen's compensation, damage, and liability
- a rider stating that all changes, whether or not they increase the cost, must be submitted and approved in writing.

Of course, this list represents the least a contract should include, but once you have signed it your plans are on the way to becoming a home.

Each set of blueprints is an interrelated collection of plans, measurements, drawings, and diagrams showing precisely how your house comes together. Here's what it includes.

Building a home? Planning a home? The Basic Blueprint Package from Home Planners, Inc., contains nearly everything you need to get the job done right, whether you're working on your own or with help from an architect, designer, builder, or subcontractors. Each Basic Blueprint Package includes detailed architect's blueprints and a specification outline.

Foundation plan. A complete basement and foundation plan in ¼-inch scale, plus a sample plot plan for locating your house on a building site.

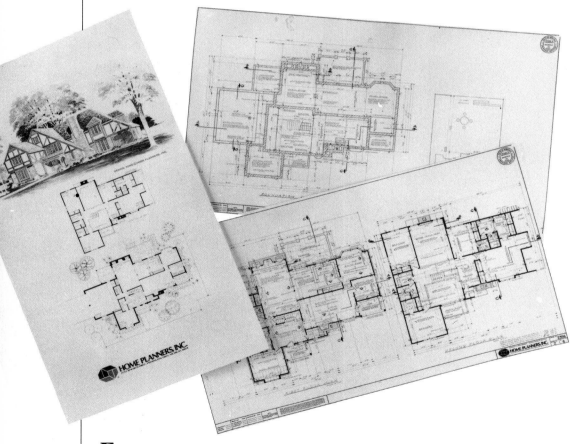

Detailed floor plans. Drawn to ¼-inch scale, each floor plan includes cross-section detail keys and layouts of electrical outlets and switches.

Frontal sheet. An artist's landscaped sketch of the exterior, along with ink-line floor plans.

TO ORDER, SEE PAGE 205

Every Basic Blueprint Package also includes a 16-page, fill-in-the-items specification list containing more than 150 stages crucial to building a house correctly, from excavating to painting. A handy guide and record, it allows you to pinpoint building materials, equipment, and methods of construction.

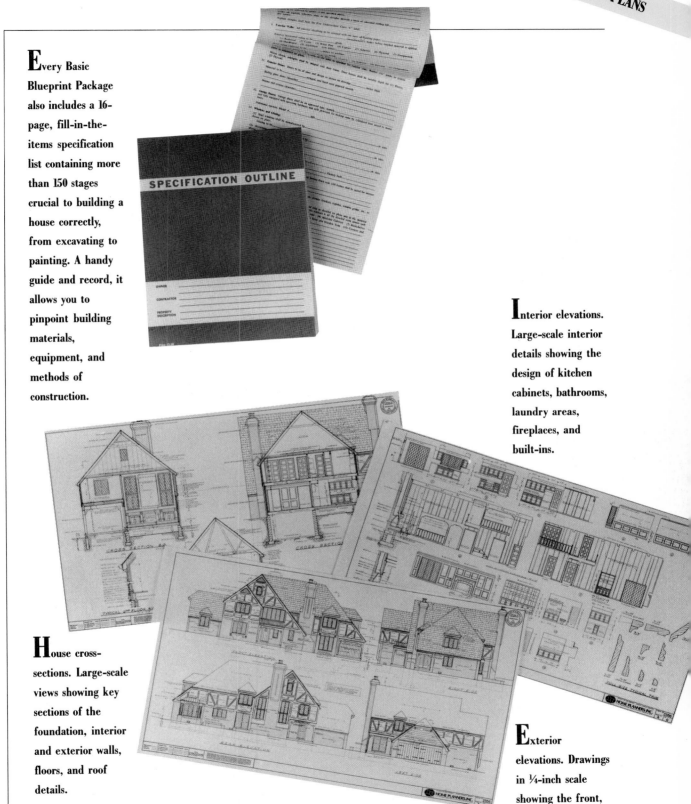

Interior elevations. Large-scale interior details showing the design of kitchen cabinets, bathrooms, laundry areas, fireplaces, and built-ins.

House cross-sections. Large-scale views showing key sections of the foundation, interior and exterior walls, floors, and roof details.

Exterior elevations. Drawings in ¼-inch scale showing the front, rear, and sides of your house.

Home Planners, Inc., offers a variety of other products aimed at helping you plan, build, and design your new home.

MATERIALS LIST

The materials list outlines the quantity, type, and size of everything needed to build your house (except mechanical materials).

Included are:

- masonry, veneer, and fireplace;
- framing lumber;
- roofing and sheet metal;
- windows and door frames;
- exterior trim and insulation;
- tile and flooring;
- interior trim;
- kitchen cabinets;
- rough and finish hardware.

The list can help you cost out materials and serve as a handy reference sheet when you're compiling bids, and help substitute building materials when you need to meet local codes, use available supplies and the like.

(Because of differing codes, our lists don't include mechanical materials and specifications. To get the necessary take-offs, consult local contractors or a local lumberyard or building supply center. Materials lists are not sold separately from the Blueprint Package.)

PLUMBING DETAILS

The Basic Blueprint Package includes locations for all the plumbing fixtures in your house, including sinks, lavatories, tubs, showers, toilets, laundry trays and water heaters. These six individual sheets —24 × 36-inch fact-packed drawings— are prepared to meet requirements of the National Plumbing Code. These valuable Plumbing Details show pipe schedules, fittings, sump-pump details, septic system details and many more. Sheets are bound together and color coded for easy reference. A glossary is included.

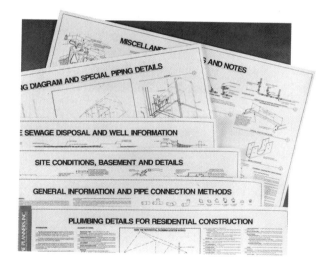

CONSTRUCTION DETAILS

The Basic Blueprint Package contains everything an experienced builder needs to construct a particular plan, but doesn't show all the different ways building materials come together to form a house, or all construction techniques used by skilled artisans. To show you a variety of additional techniques and materials, we also offer a complete set of detail drawings that depict the materials and methods used to build foundations, fireplaces, walls, floors, and roofs. Where appropriate, the drawings show acceptable alternatives. For the advanced do-it-yourselfer, owner-builder-to-be, these details are the perfect complement to the basic package.

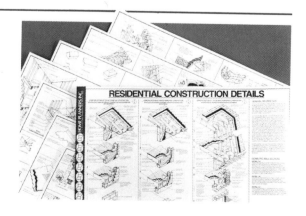

PLAN-A-HOME™

Plan-A-Home™ is a very useful tool. It's an easy-to-use product that will help you design a new home, arrange furniture in a new or existing home or plan a remodeling project. Each package contains:
• more than **700 planning symbols** on a static-cling vinyl sheet, including walls, windows, doors, furniture, kitchen components, bath fixtures, and many more. All are made of a durable, peel-and-stick vinyl you can use over and over;
• a reusable, transparent, **¼-inch-scale planning grid** that can help you create house layouts up to 140 × 92 feet;
• **tracing paper** and a protective sheet;

• a **felt-tip pen**, with water-soluble ink that wipes away quickly. The transparent planning grid matches the scale of actual working blueprints (¼ inch equals 1 foot). You can lay it over existing drawings and modify them as necessary or plan furniture arrangements before you build. Every Plan-A-Home™ package lets you lay out areas as large as a 7,500-square-foot, six-bedroom, seven-bath home. Note, however, that Plan-A-Home™ isn't meant to replace construction drawings. When you've planned a building project, consult an architect, designer, or contractor for help in developing or revising your drawings.

ELECTRICAL DETAILS

The Basic Blueprint Package shows positions for every electrical switch, plug, and outlet. However, our Electrical Details go further to take the mystery out of household electrical systems. These comprehensive 24 × 36-inch drawings come packed with helpful details. Prepared to meet requirements of the National Electrical Code, the six fact-filled sheets cover a variety of topics including appliance wattage, wire sizing, switch-installation schematics, cable-routing details, doorbell hookups, and

many others. Sheets are bound together and color coded for easy reference. A glossary of terms is also included.

Our plumbing, electrical and construction details can be remarkably useful tools. Although we don't recommend that you attempt intricate plumbing or electrical installations, or complicated building projects, these drawings will help you accomplish certain tasks and will give you and your family a thorough working knowledge with which to deal confidently with subcontractors.

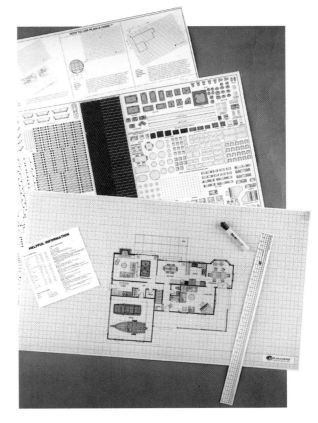

TO ORDER, SEE PAGE 205

203

THE BASIC BLUEPRINT PACKAGE

The blueprints you order are a master plan for building your new home. Even the smallest house in the Home Planners portfolio is a complicated combination of construction data and architectural detailing. Bigger houses, irregularly shaped houses, and houses with an abundance of design features are even more complex and require proportionately greater resources to plan and develop. The schedule below takes these factors into account when pricing each of the plans. When you're ready to order, note the index letter (A,B,C,D or E) next to the plan number on page 208, and refer to the prices below.

	Single Set	Four-Set Package	Eight-Set Package	Sepias
Schedule A	$125.00	$175.00	$225.00	$250.00
Schedule B	$150.00	$200.00	$250.00	$300.00
Schedule C	$175.00	$225.00	$275.00	$350.00
Schedule D	$200.00	$250.00	$300.00	$400.00
Schedule E	$300.00	$350.00	$400.00	$500.00

Additional identical Blueprints in same order: $30.00 per set.
Reverse Blueprints: $30.00 per order.
Additional Specification Outlines: $5.00 per outline.

TO ORDER FROM HOME PLANNERS' BASIC BLUEPRINT PACKAGE AND IMPORTANT EXTRAS, READ THE INFORMATION BELOW AND USE COUPON OPPOSITE.

IMPORTANT EXTRAS

Materials List (one cost for any size order) . . . . $25.00 (Schedules A–D)
$35.00 (Schedule E)

Construction Details $14.95

Plumbing Details $14.95

Electrical Details $14.95

Two-Set Package: Any Two of Construction Details, Plumbing Details, and Electrical Details . . . . $22.95 (save $6.95)

Three-Set Package: Construction Details, Plumbing Details, and Electrical Details . . . . $29.95 (save $14.90)

Plan-A-Home $24.95

BEFORE YOU ORDER

Just clip the accompanying order blank, and mail with your remittance. If you prefer, you can also use a credit card or order C.O.D. (Sorry. We aren't allowed to make C.O.D. shipments to foreign countries, including Canada.) If time is of the essence, call us. We'll ship orders received before 3 p.m. Eastern time the following day. Use this toll-free number: 1-800-521-6797. (Michigan residents call collect: 0-313-477-1850.) If you use the coupon, please note applicable postage and handling charges.

Our Service Policy
We process and ship every order from our office within 48 hours. For this reason, we won't send a formal notice acknowledging receipt of your order.

Our Exchange Policy
Because blueprints are printed in response to your order, we cannot honor requests for refunds. However, we will exchange your entire first order for an equal number of blueprints at a price of $20.00 for the first set and $10.00 for each additional set. All

sets from the previous order must be returned before the exchange can take place. Please add $3.00 for postage and handling via surface mail; $4.00 via air.

About Reverse Blueprints

If you want to build in reverse of the plan as shown, we will include upon request an extra set of reversed blueprints for an additional fee of $30.00. Although letters and dimensions appear backward, reverses will prove to be a useful visual aid if you decide to flop the plan.

Modifying Our Plans

Most contractors can make slight revisions before you start building. If you're thinking about major changes, consider ordering a set of sepias. After changes have been made on the sepia, additional sets of plans may be reproduced from the sepia master. Should you decide to revise the plan significantly, we strongly suggest that you consult an experienced architect or designer.

How Many Blueprints Do You Need?

To study your favorite house (or houses) in greater detail, one set is sufficient. On the other hand, if you plan to build, you need more. Because the first set of blueprints in each order is the scheduled price and because extra sets of the same design are only $30.00 apiece, you save a lot of money by ordering all the required sets at one time. Use the checklist below to estimate the total.

____ **Owner**

____ **Builder** (generally requires a minimum of three sets: one to use as a legal document, one to use during inspections, and at least one to give tradespeople)

____ **Community Building Department** (often requires two sets)

____ **Mortgage Lender** (to make a conventional loan, usually one set; to process government-insured or approved loans, three sets)

____ **Subdivision Committee**

____ **Planning Commission**

____ **Total Number of Sets**

To Order Blueprints By Phone

Call toll free: 1-800-521-6797.
Michigan residents call collect: 0-313-477-1850.

If we get your order by 3 p.m. Eastern time, we'll process it the same day and ship it to you from our office the following day. Call to order blueprints or books only.

Please note: When you order by phone, we'll ask for the Order Form Key. It's located in the lower left-hand corner of the order form in this section.

Canadian Customers

Please add 20% to all prices, and mail in Canadian funds to: Home Planners, Inc., 20 Cedar St. North, Kitchener, Ontario N2H 2W8
Phone: (519) 743-4169.

HOME PLANNERS, INC.,
23761 RESEARCH DRIVE
FARMINGTON HILLS, MI 48024

THE BASIC BLUEPRINT PACKAGE

Rush me the following (please refer to the Plans Index and Price Schedule in this section):

____ Set(s) of blueprints
for plan number(s) _____. $____

____ Set(s) of sepias
for plan number(s) _____. $____

____ Additional identical blueprints in same order @ $30.00 per set. $____

____ Reverse blueprints @ $30.00 per order. $____

____ Additional Specification Outlines @ $5.00 each. $____

IMPORTANT EXTRAS

Rush me the following (please refer to the Price Schedule in this section):

____ Materials List @ $25.00 (Schedules A-D) $____

____ Materials List @ $35.00 (Schedule E) $____

____ Detail Sets @ $14.95 each; any two for $22.95 (save $6.95); all three for $29.95 (save $14.90)

☐ Construction ☐ Plumbing ☐ Electrical

____ Plan-A-Home™ @ $24.95 each $____

FOR POSTAGE AND HANDLING

____ $3.00 added to order for surface mail (UPS; any merchandise) $____

____ $5.00 added for priority mail of 1-4 sets of blueprints. $____

____ $8.00 added for priority mail of 5 or more sets of blueprints $____

____ For Canadian orders, add $2.00 to applicable rates above $____

____ C.O.D. (Pay mail carrier; U.S. only)

TOTAL in U.S. funds (Michigan residents add 4% sales tax). $____

YOUR ADDRESS (please print)

Name _____

Street _____

City _____ State _____ Zip _____

Daytime telephone number (____) _____

FOR CREDIT CARD ORDERS ONLY

Please fill in the boxes below:

Credit card number   Exp. Date: Month/Year

Check one ☐   ☐

Signature

Order Form Key
TB12BP

ADDITIONAL PLANS BOOKS

THE DESIGN CATEGORY SERIES

210 ONE STORY HOMES OVER 2,000 SQUARE FEET Spacious homes for gracious living. Includes all popular styles— Spanish, Western, Tudor, French, Contemporary,  and others. Amenity-filled plans feature master bedroom suites, atriums, courtyards, and pools.

1. 192 pages. $4.95 ($5.95 Canada)

315 ONE STORY HOMES UNDER 2,000 SQUARE FEET Economical homes in a variety of styles. Efficient floor plans contain plenty of attractive fea-  tures—gathering rooms, formal and informal living and dining rooms, mudrooms, outdoor living spaces, and more. Many plans are expandable.

2. 192 pages. $4.95 ($5.95 Canada)

150 1½ STORY HOMES From starter homes to country estates. In- cludes classic story-  and-a-half styles: Contemporary, Williamsburg, Geor- gian, Tudor, and Cape Cod. Out- standing outdoor liveability. Many expandable plans.

3. 128 pages. $3.95 ($4.95 Canada)

360 TWO STORY HOMES Plans for all budgets and all families—in a wide range of styles: Tudors, Saltboxes, Farmhouses, South- ern Colonials, Geor- gians, Contempor- aries, and more. 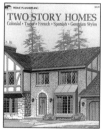 Many plans have extra-large kitchens, extra bedrooms, and extra baths.

4. 288 pages. $6.95 ($8.95 Canada)

215 MULTI-LEVEL HOMES Distinctive styles for both flat and sloping sites. Tailor-made for great outdoor living. Features include ex- posed lower levels,  upper-level lounges, balconies, decks, and terraces. Includes plans for all budgets.

5. 192 pages. $4.95 ($5.95 Canada)

223 VACATION HOMES Full-color volume features A- frames, chalets, lodges, hexagons, cottages, and other attractive styles in  one-story, two-story, and multi-level plans ranging from 480 to 3,238 square feet. Perfect for woodland, lakeside, or seashore.

6. 176 pages. $4.95 ($5.95 Canada)

THE EXTERIOR STYLE SERIES

330 EARLY AMERICAN HOME PLANS A heart-warming col- lection of the best in Early American ar- chitecture. Traces the style from colo-  nial structures to popular Traditional versions. Includes a history of styles.

7. 304 pages. $9.95 ($11.95 Canada)

335 CONTEM-PORARY HOME PLANS Required reading for anyone interested in the clean-lined elegance of Contemporary de-  sign. Features plans of all sizes and types, as well as a fascinating look at the history of this style.

8. 304 pages. $9.95 ($11.95 Canada)

136 SPANISH & WESTERN HOME DESIGNS Includes an array of sun-filled plans that emphasize indoor- outdoor livability. Key architectural  features include stucco exteriors, arches, tile roofs, wide overhangs, court- yards, terraces, patios, and more.

9. 120 pages. $3.95 ($4.95 Canada)

THE BUDGET SERIES

175 LOW BUDGET HOMES A special selection of plans for tight budgets. Offers maximum style and liveability at mini-  mum price. Includes one stories, 1½ sto- ries, two stories, and multi-levels in a range of Traditional and Contemporary styles.

10. 96 pages. $2.95 ($3.95 Canada)

165 AFFORDABLE HOME PLANS

Great plans for that first move up. Fea- tures every type of housing in a compel-  ling set of styles: Tudor, French, Early American, Spanish, and Con- temporary. Square footages start at 1,400.

11. 112 pages. $2.95 ($3.95 Canada)

142 HOME DESIGNS FOR EXPANDED BUILDING BUDGETS Spa- cious home plans for bigger families and bigger budgets aver-  age more than 2,500 square feet and en- compass all the major types and styles. Many showcase popular features including raised-hearth fireplaces and roomy kitchens.

12. 112 pages. $2.95 ($3.95 Canada)

NEW FROM HOME PLANNERS

HOME PLANS FOR OUTDOOR LIVING This superb book showcases more than 100 plans, each uniquely styled to bring the outdoors in. Features terraces, decks, porches, atriums, and sunspaces, all integrated into compelling home plans. Includes full-color photography of homes actually built and planning pointers.

13. 192 pages. $10.95 ($12.95 Canada)

COUNTRY HOUSES Shows off 80 gorgeous country homes in three styles: Cape Cods, Farmhouses, and Center-Hall Colonials. Each house features an exterior rendering, depiction of a furnished interior room, floor plans, and planning tips. Full-color section presents decorating schemes for nine country-style rooms.

14. 208 pages. $10.95 ($12.95 Canada)

HOME PLANS FOR SOLAR LIVING This book proves that passive solar design can be stylish and practical. One hundred home plans feature a detailed floor plan, rendering of the elevation, and notes on siting the design. Includes a helpful introduction to solar floor planning and a gallery of color photos that shows how gorgeous these sun-drenched homes can be!

15. 192 pages. $10.95 ($12.95 Canada)

PLAN PORTFOLIOS

ENCYCLOPEDIA OF HOME DESIGNS (450 PLANS) The largest book of its kind— 450 plans in a complete range of housing types, styles, and sizes. Includes plans for all building budgets, families, and styles of living.

16. 320 pages. $9.95 ($11.95 Canada)

MOST POPULAR HOME DESIGNS (360 PLANS) Our customers' favorite plans, including one-story, 1½ story, two-story, and multi-level homes in a variety of styles. For families large and small. Designs feature many of today's most popular features: lounges, clutter rooms, sunspaces, media rooms, and more.

17. 272 pages. $8.95 ($10.95 Canada)

Please fill out the coupon below. We will process your order and ship it from our office within 48 hours. Send coupon and check for the total to:

HOME PLANNERS, INC.
23761 Research Drive, Department BK
Farmington Hills, MI 48024

THE DESIGN CATEGORY SERIES
1. _____ 210 One Story Homes over 2,000 Square Feet @ $4.95 ($5.95 Canada) $_____
2. _____ 315 One Story Homes Under 2,000 Square Feet @ $4.95 ($5.95 Canada) $_____
3. _____ 150 1½ Story Homes @ $3.95 ($4.95 Canada) $_____
4. _____ 360 Two Story Homes @ $6.95 ($8.95 Canada) $_____
5. _____ 215 Multi-Level Homes @ $4.95 ($5.95 Canada) $_____
6. _____ 223 Vacation Homes @ $4.95 ($5.95 Canada) $_____

THE EXTERIOR STYLE SERIES
7. _____ 330 Early American Home Plans @ $9.95 ($11.95 Canada) $_____
8. _____ 335 Contemporary Home Plans @ $9.95 ($11.95 Canada) $_____
9. _____ 136 Spanish & Western Home Designs @ $3.95 ($4.95 Canada) $_____

THE BUDGET SERIES
10. _____ 175 Low Budget Homes @ $2.95 ($3.95 Canada) $_____
11. _____ 165 Affordable Home Plans @ $2.95 ($3.95 Canada) $_____
12. _____ 142 Home Designs for Expanded Building Budgets @ $2.95 ($3.95 Canada) $_____

NEW FROM HOME PLANNERS
13. _____ Home Plans for Outdoor Living @ $10.95 ($12.95 Canada) $_____
14. _____ Country Houses @ $10.95 ($12.95 Canada) $_____
15. _____ Home Plans for Solar Living @ $10.95 ($12.95 Canada) $_____

PLAN PORTFOLIOS
16. _____ Encyclopedia of Home Designs @ $9.95 ($11.95 Canada) $_____
17. _____ Most Popular Home Designs @ $8.95 ($10.95 Canada) $_____

Sub total $_____
Michigan residents: Add 4% sales tax $_____
Add postage and handling $ 1.50
TOTAL (please enclose check) $_____

Name (please print) _____
Address _____
City _____ State _____ Zip _____

CANADIAN CUSTOMERS: Please use Canadian prices noted. Remit in Canadian funds to: Home Planners, Inc., 20 Cedar St. North, Kitchener, Ontario N2H 2W8 Phone: (519) 743-4169

TB12BK

TO ORDER BY PHONE CALL TOLL FREE: 1-800-521-6797
MICHIGAN RESIDENTS CALL COLLECT: 0-313-477-1850

PLANS AND BLUEPRINT PRICE INDEX

PLAN NO.	PAGE	PRICE SCHEDULE
C1988	174	C
C1989	80	C
C1991	86	B
C2126	122	B
C2128	68	B
C2129	70	B
C2137	92	B
C2141	146	C
C2142	116	C
C2148	160	C
C2151	98	A
C2170	50	B
C2171	64	B
C2206	48	B
C2218	136	C
C2239	162	C
C2241	148	C
C2242	76	B
C2243	156	C
C2245	180	D
C2254	158	C
C2263	78	B
C2278	88	C
C2317	176	D
C2318	66	B
C2324	120	B
C2354	90	C
C2356	184	D
C2366	60	A
C2373	84	B
C2374	58	B
C2391	178	C
C2508	172	C
C2541	164	C
C2565	40	B
C2568	150	C
C2570	36	A
C2573	132	C
C2577	142	C
C2586	102	A
C2589	138	C
C2604	56	B
C2606	38	A
C2607	34	A
C2613	72	B
C2624	114	B
C2626	106	B
C2629	126	B
C2637	110	B
C2674	134	C
C2678	62	B
C2728	54	B
C2732	108	B
C2737	52	B
C2746	140	C
C2758	130	C
C2785	112	C
C2788	128	B
C2794	166	C
C2800	100	B
C2802	46	B
C2806	44	B
C2825	42	B
C2829	182	D
C2844	152	C
C2847	94	C
C2854	82	B
C2855	124	B
C2939	118	B
C2951	194	E
C2953	188	E
C2954	190	E
C2955	196	E
C2957	186	D
C2958	154	C
C2959	104	B
C2960	170	B
C2961	144	D
C2962	74	B
C2968	192	E

TO ORDER, SEE FORM ON PAGE 205.